FINDING THE LOV

FINDING THE LOVE
OF YOUR LIFE

LINDA SONNTAG

PICCADILLY PRESS • LONDON

The right of Linda Sonntag to be identified as Author
of this work has been asserted by her in accordance
with the Copyright, Designs and Patents Act 1988.

Phototypeset by First Impressions, Lingfield, Surrey
Printed and bound by Biddles Ltd., Guildford, Surrey
for the publisher
Piccadilly Press Ltd.,
5 Castle Road, London NW1 8PR

A catalogue record for this book is available from the
British Library

ISBN 1-85340-260-5

Linda Sonntag is British. She has had a number of
very entertaining dating experiences, and has lived to
tell the tales. She has written a number of books
including *Making Love,* which is now on video.

This is her first book for Piccadilly Press.

CONTENTS

Acknowledgements

I should like to thank all the introduction agencies who supplied me with information for this book, and all their members who spoke to me, whose names I have of course changed.

For their particular help, I'd like to thank Mary Balfour of Drawing Down the Moon; Penrose Halson of the Katharine Allen Marriage Bureau; Jeremy Wright of The Picture Dating Agency; Frances Pyne of Dateline International; Jennifer Stacey of Friendships; and Barbara Bradshaw of Natural Friends.

Note

Addresses of agencies and cost of membership at the time of writing are to be found on page 174.

Dedication

I'd like to dedicate this book to the 62 intelligent, attractive, caring, considerate, sensitive men who answered my adverts.

INTRODUCTION

About a year ago I found myself wishing that I had more single male friends. I thought it probably didn't help that I was living in the depths of the countryside, but in fact my single female friends in London were afflicted with a similar dearth of unattached men. *"Have you tried advertising?"* I asked them, *"or ever thought of joining an introduction agency?"* No, they most definitely had not. The very idea made them curl up with horror and revulsion, but at the same time, they were strangely fascinated. Aha! I thought, this is something that people want to know more about, but preferably first from the snug privacy of their fireside armchairs - it would make a good subject for a book! But, of course, before I could write about it, I had to try it myself.

The first thing I had to face was my own prejudice: I had a feeling that to set out deliberately to meet people must mean admitting you were a social failure or an emotional wreck. So I went straight away to see Mary Balfour, who runs Britain's best known introduction agency, Drawing Down the Moon. Here I discovered the reasons why busy young professionals are increasingly using the services of reputable matchmakers to find themselves mates. As I was a busy no-longer-quite-so-young professional, Mary encouraged me to try advertising. Advertising is a cheaper and quicker and less predictable method of making contacts than joining an agency, where a lot of the initial filtering out is done for you. During the course of writing this book I came across many advertisers and agency members for whom the experiment had worked; my own experiences I would describe as "novel". However, the message of this book is not that this is an infallible method of searching out and finding love and happiness, but that it is alright to try it. As society gets more and more fragmented, I am sure it will become a more obvious and acceptable way of getting in touch.

I hope this book will encourage you to plug into the network of single people and see who lights up. Even if you don't meet anyone who changes your life, you will have changed your life yourself, by opening it up to new experience.

Chapter One

OH, NO, HAS IT COME TO THIS?

The thought of advertising for a partner or joining an agency makes some people cringe. They think of it as an admission of failure. If it has come to this, they say, you must be on the shelf and way past your expiry date, reduced to casting in your lot with any other social misfit desperate enough to have you.

My investigation of Britain's top introduction agencies, and my own practical research as a guinea pig among the lonely hearts columns of our national newspapers, have proved to me that this is simply not true, and my purpose in writing this book is to clear up some of the misconceptions about this enterprising way of getting together, and to encourage more people to try it.

Did you know that there's an agency that caters for people who are too glamorous and successful to find love? Are you aware that there are many agencies whose members are mostly graduates, working in medicine, law, business and the arts? Have you ever realized how difficult it must be for a man or woman in the public eye - say a television presenter or a politician - who is surrounded by sycophantic admirers, to find someone who likes the person behind the image? Have you wondered how people who work long or unsociable hours, such as doctors, actors and restaurateurs, or who spend a lot of time travelling, as do business people, journalists and diplomats, ever meet anyone other than people they work with? People in all these lines of work use agencies to help them find a partner because the service is discreet and selective.

There are many reasons why a single person with an attractive personality, an interesting job and plenty of friends, can find it very difficult to meet compatible people of the opposite sex. Firstly, today's society is highly mobile, and while it is easy to leave the community you live in, it takes time and effort to make your place in the one you move into. Past generations stayed put among family and friends and married people they probably knew, or knew of, as children, but today fewer of us belong to long established networks of relationships, so these are less likely to introduce a partner.

Specialization also takes us farther away from each other. People whose jobs are important to them like to be able to share the excitement and frustrations of their work with their partners, but for most, this does not mean marrying a colleague, a client or a patient. For reasons of professional etiquette or ethics, workplace romances are usually ruled out, and business kept separate from pleasure. And of course, many jobs involve either working alone, or working mainly with members of your own sex. People who are absorbed in their careers often realize only quite late that all their friends have been busy pairing off while they were still hard at work.

For women who have always thought that one day they would like to have children, the realization that they are still single and already in their mid- or late thirties can cause sudden alarm. With their biological clock beginning to run down, they feel they must meet someone soon, but are aware that being under pressure could lead to a hasty wrong decision. Women of this age who are highly successful in their chosen professions are very difficult to please. They not unnaturally hope to find partners with similar achievements to their credit, but statistics show that the few women who do get to the top in management do so at the expense of a private life, whereas their male counterparts tend to be married, probably to women who are content to play a traditional supportive role.

It is always comforting to remember, however, that Mel Gibson found his wife through a dating agency.

WHAT ARE THE PROSPECTS?

So now you know you're not alone in being

single, what are the prospects for getting together? First, here are some statistics. Approximately 6 per cent more boys than girls are born each year, but more men than women die each year, and women live longer than men, so this creates an imbalance in the population at either end of the age range. There are many more men than women under the age of 25, and many more women than men over the age of 55. In generations affected by war, there is also obviously a dearth of men. Most, but not all, agencies find it more difficult to match women over 40 and men under 30. Most agencies - but again there are exceptions - have more women than men on their books.

Mary Balfour of Drawing Down the Moon has more women, and explains this by saying that while there are biological and social pressures on a woman to find a partner, society works against men committing themselves, and men who want to play the field don't usually need to join an agency to do so. Jennifer Stacey of Friendships agrees that women are keener on domestic togetherness, but her agency has a superfluity of men. She says this is because many divorced women are too busy bringing up their children to look for a new man, while divorced men often have time and money on their hands and put it to good use meeting new women. Drawing Down the Moon is one of the most expensive agencies, so the men who join it are likely to be serious in their search for a permanent partner, and there are fewer of this sort about. Friendships is very reasonably priced, and therefore has more men who are less serious about commitment. But, of course, men can and do change their minds.

A good agency will give you a frank opinion of your prospects with their clients. It is after all in their interest to do so, as many new members come recommended by word of mouth, and a reputation for fair dealing is essential for good business. Mary Balfour advised me against joining Drawing Down the Moon, because I lived outside the area that her agency caters for. However, she would still have dissuaded me had I lived in the heart of London, and her reasons astonished me.

Firstly, there was my age. At 41, I stood little chance of being chosen by many of her male members, who are more often than not looking for women with whom they could start a family in a few years' time. Secondly, there was the fact that I wear glasses. I was utterly amazed that this should go against me, especially in an agency that advertised itself as being for "thinking people".

"But surely some thinking men wear glasses themselves?" I expostulated. *"They must realize that my glasses do come off - they're not bolted to my head. And anyway, I like my glasses."*

Mary, who ironically enough at this point had something in her eye and was having trouble with her contact lens, agreed that there were distinct advantages to wearing glasses. But she explained that, much as she would like her men to be unprejudiced about age and eyewear, her members were representative of the population at large, and unfortunately men at large, even educated men in their forties with top jobs who wore glasses themselves, preferred to meet younger women who did not wear glasses. It was unfair, but with a larger selection of women on her books, the men could and did call the tune.

A further revelation was in store. When I asked Mary's opinion of the photograph I had had taken, she frowned and said dubiously: *"Men don't like women with things on their heads. This hat, or whatever it is - they won't like it."*

Actually, it was a black and white spotted headband, and I had thought the effect rather Parisian. Never mind: this was a remarkable piece of information, and I wondered how Mary had come by it. She told me that she had learned it quite simply from her observation. The men who come into her office to leaf through the files pay particular attention to the photographs of women attached, and the ones wearing "things on their heads" are more often than not passed over. It seems that hats, headbands, scarves and hair ornaments are a definite turn-off. I asked my male friends about this and uncovered a definite dislike of Alice bands and a feeling that hats can look very striking on women, *"but I wouldn't want to go out with a woman who was wearing one.*"

What can be behind this strange phenomenon? Here is my theory. Hats enlarge and draw attention to the head, and the "head" is the one in charge. Women who want to make an impression are often advised: *"If you want to get ahead, get a hat.*" Men take off their hats as an act of deference, making their heads appear smaller and vulnerable. So men feel their authority is undermined by a woman in a hat. A man likes a woman to be vulnerable, so that he can be in charge, or, to put it more kindly, in charge of protecting her. Alice bands, hair ornaments, glasses - any "things on their heads" - make women seem less accessible and less vulnerable. Think how many films there are in which the heroine's beauty and sexuality are only fully revealed when the hero pulls the pins out of her hair and takes off her glasses to kiss her.

Personally, I'm all for a hero who has the imagination and intelligence to be able to see through a pair of glasses, and who thinks, like I do, that hats can be amusing, as well as useful for keeping in the 20 per cent of body heat that is said to escape through your head if you don't wear one on a cold day. But, I asked Mary Balfour, would there be any hope for a woman of my advanced years with such odd opinions?

Mary answered in the affirmative, and she advised me to try advertising. Her advice was very good, and she saved me a lot of money as well as disappointment. You can read the results of my experiment on page 23.

The point to remember is that there are many different avenues you can take in your search for compatible people. If someone advises you honestly that you would not fit with the people on her books, don't take it as a reflection on your own shortcomings. All it means is that this agency is not right for you. There are agencies for everyone - smart people, green people, country people, disabled people. Lots extend a warm welcome to single parents. Don't throw away your Alice band unless you want to: look elsewhere, where people will accept you for what you are. You want to meet people you're comfortable with, not people you're trying desperately to please all the time.

There are many hundreds - possibly even thousands - of dating agencies all over the country, but because of restrictions of space, I have had to be selective. I have concentrated therefore on the agencies that are members of the Association of British Introduction Agencies, an umbrella body that protects its members' clients. Look in the phone book and the local paper for other agencies near you, but take note of the recommendations on page 73 before joining.

A new type of agency, video dating, has yet to find its way into the ABIA. If you can talk about yourself naturally in front of a camera, and would like to see videos of other people doing the same before you make up your mind about meeting them, then this could be an interesting option. An audio equivalent for advertisers is teledating, and you can find out about both by looking in the back of a magazine such as *Time Out*. Here you read the personal ad, then ring a phone number to listen to a recorded message of the advertiser telling you about himself or herself. If you like what you hear, you can leave a reply and your own phone number.

I rang a couple of teledating numbers fom the back of *Private Eye*, inviting them to ring me back and help with the research for this book. Unfortunately, I got no response! The man I rang mumbled uninvitingly about his guitar and his dog, but the woman was oozing with confidence: she described herself as a tall, slim bisexual redhead with green eyes and a PhD in sex.

There's a nationwide agency called Nexus (see the Yellow Pages to find the number of a branch in your area), which though not a member of the ABIA, deserves a mention here because of its different approach. I spoke to Susan, who had joined for six months at a cost of around £50, which entitled her to listen to taped messages like those above, but vetted by the agency. Each message had a code number, and Susan rang Nexus with the code, and was given the telephone number of the person whose message had appealed to her.

Each telephone introduction is logged by the agency to provide clients with a measure of safety. Susan found the experience interesting, though she said it was very difficult to judge from a voice alone whether you wanted to meet a person. Of course, the initial telephone call can be followed by an exchange of letters and photographs.

As yet, there are no agencies for gays or lesbians within the ABIA, but several do exist. Look in a publication such as *Gay News* for details, and to find about gay and lesbian clubs and events in your area. It's also worth checking the lonely hearts column of your local paper, as gay and lesbian personal ads are becoming much more of a feature in the non-specialist press.

EXPLORING OTHER AVENUES

As you get older, your circle of friends tends to decrease. Single people often lose touch with married friends once they become absorbed with babies. You become more discriminating, and your most important friendships deepen into lifelong bonds. It is easy to rely on a handful of good close friendships, but if you're hoping to meet a partner, you have to reverse the trend and widen your social circle.

There are organizations especially for single people that will help you to do this. In London, for example, London Village (071 586 7455), Breakaway (081 991 2169) and Kaleidoscope (081 997 7994) hold events all over the capital at which you can meet people who share your special interest, whether it's an evening in a pub or wine bar, jazz, folk, squash, ballroom dancing or art history. The Intervarsity Club (IVC, 071 240 0487) has branches nationwide and offers similar activities to graduates and professional people (not that the other organizations exclude them). Paul Brennan, the administrator of IVC's Covent Garden branch, stressed to me that IVC is not a dating agency or a marriage bureau, and not strictly for single people. However, he then revealed that he'd met his wife on an IVC holiday in

Berlin, which I said certainly qualified IVC for a recommendation in this book. Ring for the brochures to see the variety of activities on offer.

Supper clubs are springing up in major cities and towns. Some are quite expensive, and offer a well-heeled clientele multi-course meals in exclusive restaurants, the idea being that the parties are hand-picked and one sex moves a couple of seats round the table after each course, so that you all get the chance to talk to everyone else of the opposite sex. Less expensive suppers may be held in Greek or Italian restaurants, where the wine, the music and the relaxed atmosphere encourage high spirits and camaraderie. One club I contacted offered to organize a party of a dozen people to come for dinner in your own house, with the club's president as host. This seemed to me a horrendous idea: in addition to paying for the privilege of welcoming a group of strangers into your home, you were expected to provide them with food and drink, and do the washing -up afterwards.

For people who prefer a less head-on approach to widening their circle of friends, the best way is often to involve yourself in the activities of your immediate community. Mary Balfour of Drawing Down the Moon told me that most of the successful relationships that come into bud at her agency are formed between people living within a distance of eight miles of each other. This does not surprise me, as the process of getting to know someone can follow its own natural rhythm when you are only a few minutes away by car, bus or bicycle; a greater distance necessitates planning and makes spontaneous meetings impractical.

So go to your local library, museum, art gallery, town hall, health food shop or bookshop, and pick up leaflets or study the posters to see what's on. Talks are easier to attend than dances if you are going on your own. Evening classes are always a good idea, especially if you pick a course that has an element of participation, such as learning a new language. Choose electrical engineering rather than flowercraft if you want to meet men. Local council or parish meetings can be fascinating, and have the added advantage that you, as a member of the community, have a right to attend, and to contribute to matters that concern you. Similarly, local political party meetings may provide lively discussion that you can take part in. And if you have skills that qualify you to run a group or a course yourself, or to join a choir or a band, this can offer another way of meeting local people.

After all this effort, you'll need a holiday - see page 144.

The Rendezvous: Starting A Test-Tube Relationship

Whether you make contact through an ad or an agency, you should already know quite a bit about the person you are going to meet before you make the date, so he or she will no longer be a complete stranger. You will have gathered information and formed impressions from an exchange of photographs and letters, or from an agency profile of your prospective partner, and from talking to each other on the phone.

For your comfort and safety, always arrange to meet for the first time in a public place on neutral territory where you can be among but not with other people; somewhere with a relaxed atmosphere, such as a wine bar. Some women also like to tell a friend where they have gone and whom they are meeting, and some will not divulge their address until they have met, preferring to keep in contact on the phone or by letter via the agency. Too much wariness can offend, but it is sensible to make your own travel arrangements, and not to allow your date to pick you up or take you back home, just in case he or she turns out to be a pest. Of course, it's unlikely that you'll meet a pest through an agency, especially one with a personal service, because you would be able to complain and the pest could be struck off the books.

Meeting in a place that offers plenty of distraction can set you at your ease, and if you agree to meet for just a drink, it offers each of you the chance of an early getaway without offending, should the other person not appeal. First meetings are best kept to half an hour or so, and it's a good idea to make this plain before you meet.

Meeting a prospective partner is bound to make you nervous, and the first time you do it your expectations may be unrealistically high. But it does get easier, especially when you realize that the other person is nervous too. If you feel dreadful, say so: it breaks the tension.

Starting a "test-tube relationship" is different from meeting people in the ordinary course of events. Some people say it's like starting a relationship halfway through. Although you are virtual strangers, certain personal questions need to be asked and answered. There can be a sense of the surreal, because this is one of the few social situations in which complete honesty is allowable. It certainly calls for kindness, tact and strength: strength to reject and to take rejection oneself. You have to be at the same time more open, and more in control.

The success of the first meeting may not always be obvious. If you feel unsure of the other person's opinion, wait for a few days and then write a note suggesting that you get together again: this is much easier than risking a rejection in person or on the telephone.

WHAT IF IT WORKS - DO YOU TELL YOUR FRIENDS?

Of course there is no guarantee that you will fall in love, but using agencies and adverts will undoubtedly increase your opportunities for meeting the right person. Patience and perseverance are recommended by agency staff and members alike. I did speak to someone who was celebrating two years of living with the first woman who replied to his advert in *Private Eye*, but to strike lucky so spectacularly must be unusual.

My own experiment with advertising was a fascinating episode in my life, introducing novelty and a spirit of adventure, because each man I met was so very different from the next in character, outlook and experience. Meeting new people always has unexpected benefits: one man, a member of the Katharine Allen marriage bureau, said that the sheer variety of women he had met had made him more tolerant.

If eventually you do find the right partner, and you begin to be introduced to each other's friends, they are bound to ask you where you met. If you tell them, they will probably be surprised, fascinated, and avid for details. Some people choose to tell; others don't. Those who pretend they met at a party or walking the dog say that it's no one else's business but their own. Those who tell their close friends and family (and after all, no one else is likely to ask), say that after the initial rush of curiosity, the way they met becomes irrelevant - just as it would be if they had met at a party or walking the dog.

When they are told, people tend to be full of curious surprise because they never imagined you had any problem meeting the opposite sex.

They won't have thought through the points made at the beginning of this introduction. Neither will they have reasoned to themselves, as you have, that in a world where we are used to employing professionals - lawyers and accountants, hairdressers and homeopaths, even orthodontists, psychiatrists and interior designers - to employ a specialist in the field of matchmaking is just another sensible executive decision. You will probably think it the best one you ever made.

Chapter Two

DISCREET, DESIRABLE, DARING OR DESPERATE? CONTACT A BOX NUMBER AND CHANGE YOUR LIFE

Lonely hearts advertisements were as popular in eighteenth and nineteenth-century Britain as they are today, and at one time there were three journals devoted solely to the marriage market: *The Marriage Gazette, The Matrimonial Journal,* and *Nuptials.* Marriage partners were also sought in other periodicals; here is an advertisement discovered by Mary Balfour of Drawing Down the Moon in the *Gazetteer* of 1839:

"Matrimony. A gentleman of rank, a Protestant, and possessing an income of a thousand pounds, is desirous of a union with an accomplished young lady of suitable age, and whose station in society and connections are at least on a par with his own."

In those days rank and fortune were the main criteria by which a good match was judged. As recently as 1950, romance was still not a priority between partners, and a survey showed that people considered decency, respectability and financial security to be the principal ingredients of a successful marriage. It is only over the last few decades that personal compatibility has become generally acknowledged as the most important factor in choosing a partner.

Personal compatibility is more difficult to assess through a column of newsprint than financial or social status, but more of us are trying it every year, and now even *The Times* and *The Guardian* devote space to matchmaking.

I was assured by Mary Balfour that advertising is much the best hope for a woman over 40 looking for a partner. In fact placing an ad in the personal columns guarantees that whatever your age, you will get noticed straight away by the large numbers of people who regularly browse through the lonely hearts because they make irresistible reading. There is an element of the voyeur in all of us. Personal columns are almost as fascinating as agony pages for the light they throw on other people's lives, and they have the added attraction of offering adventure: just contacting a box number could change your life.

Advertising is generally much cheaper than joining an agency, and another advantage is that you get a much faster response - hopefully from several applicants at once. A box number guarantees complete confidentiality. You can decide what to say about yourself - good for people who hate filling in forms and can never remember what their hobbies are - and you can decide how, or even whether, to reply to the letters that you get.

WHERE TO ADVERTISE

Advertise in the magazine or newspaper that you read yourself. That way you will reach people with similar outlook, background, interests and political views.

If you can afford it, advertise in several places at once. Try varying your advert to suit the paper you are placing it in. This multi-pronged approach will attract different types of prospective partner. I advertised in five places at once and was inundated with replies. Broadly speaking, my *Guardian* correspondents tended to be thoughtful, wear comfortable clothes and have arts-related jobs, while more of my *Sunday Times* contacts were dynamic, money-orientated, and in business or computers. I also advertised in the *Times, New Statesman and Society* and the *Spectator*. I had very few replies from the last two, probably because my advert was too frivolous. Check with the style of the other adverts before you place yours. In all I had over 50 replies, about half from *The Guardian*, the rest divided more or less equally between the other two.

WHAT TO PUT?

It can be surprisingly difficult trying to word an original and eyecatching advert that says something about yourself and the person you would like to meet without being outlandish or boastful.

I rang Mary Balfour and read her my advert: *"Writer, 41 ... "*

"No good," she said, *"absolutely not. A woman should never reveal her age. Just state the age of the man you're looking for. "*

That was one piece of good advice, and I followed it. I took up her other recommendation more reluctantly.

"You haven't put 'attractive'," she said. *"Why not?"*

I said that 'attractive' existed only in the eye of the beholder. *"I can't say I'm attractive. "*

"You're being too scrupulous," said Mary. *"Put it in. Otherwise they'll think you look like the back of a bus. "*

My own study of the small ads in local and national papers and magazines confirmed how important it is to include the word "attractive". There is one striking difference between what male and female advertisers say they are looking for. Most women invite response from men with warm personal attributes, such as kindness, sensitivity and generosity. Most men want these too but more often than not specify something else besides: good looks.

Male concern with appearance can be both daunting and off-putting to the woman considering the personal columns. What women least like about the whole dating and matchmaking business is the feeling that they're lining up at a beauty show, competing for male attention.

Of course appearance is important to both sexes when it comes to falling in love, but not as the embodiment of vital statistics. Appearance is important as an expression of the chemistry of attraction, and personal chemistry can overturn everyone's ideals and prejudices at the meeting of two pairs of eyes. Men will get a better response to their adverts if they don't give a physical description of their ideal woman, and they will stand a more realistic chance of meeting a partner if they keep an open mind about what she might look like. Women will undoubtedly get more replies if they describe themselves as attractive.

Frances Pyne of Dateline sent me the results of a survey conducted among the readers of *Dateline Magazine* in an attempt to discover how people respond to singles adverts. "Attractive" was the third most important attribute that readers looked for. "Sense of humour" got the most positive response, with "caring" second. Other high-scoring adjectives were "loving", "sincere", "professional", "intelligent", "genuine", "romantic", "lonely", "shy", "slim", "non-smoking" and "graduate".

Big turn-offs for Dateline readers were "fat", "smoking", "wealthy", "sexy", "handsome" and "funloving", and many cringed at any mention of "hunk", "gent", "refined", "cultured" and "loves cuddles".

Dateline is the only organization that keeps records of how well its advertisers do, and

Frances Pyne sent me copies of their most popular ads.

DATELINE'S MOST POPULAR PERSONAL ADS

Sensual, imaginative brunette, 25, artistic, intelligent, with a sense of humour, enjoys: home life, cooking, sports, country life; no ties, own home. Seeking a tall, strong, intelligent, fun companion, with inner depth, for passionate, loving romance, 25-35. Photo guarantees reply. Must feel able to love Ben my dog too. Midlands/ anywhere.

- 241 replies forwarded

Very lonely Auxiliary nurse, 31, full of love, shy, romantic, SOH [sense of humour], *anxiously hoping for a letter from you, ALA* [all letters answered].

- 230 replies forwarded

Wanted: single, sincere, good humoured, faithful man, 25-52, to save this London-based single girl from a lifetime of early nights and cocoa! I'm 23, 5ft 5in tall, of medium build, with auburn hair and green eyes, good sense of humour, sincere and faithful. Interested in a variety of things - music, history and science fiction being some. I'd love to hear from you. Photo appreciated, but not essential, mine in return. London or further afield, as I'm prepared to travel if you are.

- 229 replies forwarded

Affectionate architect, 49, divorced, 6ft 2in, slim, tall, presentable; caring, loving, unpretentious and kind, yearns to pamper an affectionate feminine female, and together enjoy all that life has to offer, but most importantly each other. From dancing in the dark to drying the dishes, or sunbathing in the Seychelles to shopping at Sainsbury's, sharing makes everything worthwhile. Let's make this the year we

31

*started sharing our lives together?
Photograph appreciated. Home counties
area.*

- 181 replies forwarded

*Space in my heart. Lady, 36, outgoing,
easygoing, goodlooking, sexy, adorable,
willing to relocate for someone. Age
immaterial. Intelligent, considerate,
generous and loyal.*

- 165 replies forwarded

*Last dream, last hope, last endeavour.
True love to enrich final phase of life.
English male, 53, retiring soon, casts his
fate to the winds. Attractive, it's said, 5ft
10in tall, greying too. At least some of the
things you like. Pisces (good catch?).
There's more, let me tell you. Last love,
where are you?*

- 160 replies forwarded

Stephanie - Kentish lady, 43, divorced, 3 daughters grown, 2 flown, writer, artist, nature lover, country girl, homemaker, vulnerable, penniless, looking for love, home, security. Photo appreciated, returned. Non-smoker.

- 145 replies forwarded

Anne, very attractive, sensitive, intelligent brunette, 33, looking for friendship/love/ marriage. Photo ensures reply. You are sincere, attractive, 30-39. London/ anywhere.

- 144 replies forwarded

Special lady needed. This 6ft tall, slim, presentable, well dressed, not unattractive man has many friends, but lacks a very special lady in his life. I'm divorced, financially secure with my own home in Central London, happy in my rewarding and interesting management career, and enjoying a relaxed lifestyle. If you're around 40, slim, reasonably attractive, romantic, caring, shy, and in need of warmth, affection and loyalty, you could be the special lady to fulfil my life. I'm a very young-at-heart 52, with a good sense of humour, and like music - from rock to classical - good restaurants, theatre, cinema, tv, sports, travel abroad, English villages, country pubs, conversation, togetherness, and romantic evenings by the fire. Why not send a brief note with a telephone number so we can talk, and see what happens? I would like a photograph please, which I promise faithfully to return immediately, with one of myself. Please don't put it off - we may both be missing the best thing that ever happened to us!

- 144 replies forwarded

Warm natured director, divorced, 1st time advertiser, very young 58, presentable, active, well read, well travelled, beautiful house/garden (South London), great sense of humour, lots of TLC for Mrs Right. Wishes to meet elegant lady, 50-58, genuinely affectionate, with no hang-ups from previous marriage, attractive, dresses well, enjoys: travel locally/abroad, and intelligent conversation, n/s [non-smoker], to share my life, home, to drink with me from the cup of life to the last drop and sail away to everlasting happiness, of which there will be plenty, if the chemistry is right. Recent photo returnable, and phone number.

- 143 replies forwarded

If you don't like writing about yourself in glowing terms, get a friend to do it for you. "I'm looking for an interesting man to introduce to my stunningly beautiful cousin," sounds more acceptable than claiming to be a ravishing belle yourself.

I chose to describe myself as "piquant", and an unusual word proved to be a good idea, because almost all my respondents commented on it. Several had even looked it up in the dictionary and wanted to know which kind of "piquant" I was: "having an agreeably pungent or tart taste", "lively or stimulating to the mind" or "cutting and severe". (I said I had the potential for all three.)

It seems a shame that few people mention their occupation in adverts, though men often give their status: "successful company director", for instance. Women who don't want to frighten men with their success put "professional". Perhaps advertisers are afraid of being found out by their colleagues, or think their jobs sound boring, but an indication of the area in which you work can say a lot about your personality.

As for leisure interests, it seems that both sexes like the same things: country walks, music, theatre, holidays abroad, eating in or out and sharing a bottle of wine in front of a roaring log fire. Be realistic. Do you have a roaring log fire? Don't be tempted to say that you like the theatre when what you mean is that you like the idea of it, but that in fact you haven't been for 20 years. I met one man who described himself as "fit, a lover of sport and travel". It turned out that he was a chain smoker who watched football on TV. As for travel, he hadn't been anywhere since he was nine.

Finally, there is the question of location. Advertising nationally and not specifying where you live will get you a bigger response, but how practical is it to travel across half the country each weekend? How desirable is it to spend huge chunks of time with a person you hardly know? It can feel unnatural, because in the normal course of things, relationships are built up gradually over a long period. Travelling is expensive, time-consuming and tiring, and will soon help you decide how much you like someone. On the other hand, refusing to travel might immediately cut out the very person you wouldn't mind crawling on hands and knees to Australia to see.

How To Place Your Ad

First find out how much it will cost. Write out your ad (some periodicals provide a printed form for you to fill in and cut out). Send it in with your cheque, making sure of course that your own name and address are clearly legible.

Always ask for a box number for privacy and to protect yourself from nuisance callers. Find out how long the box number stays open. Some people wait weeks before making up their minds to reply.

The easiest and quickest way of placing your ad is over the phone: dictate the ad and pay by card. You could be opening your first letter within days.

And The Replies Come Flooding In ...

For six weeks after I advertised, the replies kept coming through my letter box. It was exciting to find a fat brown envelope full of men on my mat every morning, and all so every different from one another. I was entertained, touched, amazed and intrigued. There were poems, photographs of cornflowers and French churches (as well as men), an illuminated letter the size of a tea towel, autobiographies and scrawled telephone numbers on otherwise empty sheets of paper. As it was December, there were Christmas cards, some of them home-made. I had letters from places as far apart as Stroud and the Bahamas, as well as one from on board the QE2. The whole experience was very cheering. There were countless interesting single men out there lighting up the map.

I could discount some of the letter-writers straight away, but this didn't mean their letters weren't worth receiving. There was D, for instance, bemused to find himself at the tail end of his marriage and choosing curtains for a home of his own. The shock of his separation had made mundane events take on surreal significance: he described the slow-motion feeling of falling off his bike into a ditch, drunk but uncannily sober. We wrote to each other several times, though I ruled out D because he was still untangling himself from his wife.

Two letter writers addressed me as *"Dear madam"*, and one as *"Hello babe!"*, while my

Bermudan correspondent began: *"Well, hello there, you seem to be a nice kind of girl."* A psychologist with smooth and regular writing wanted to share a bottle of claret (this sounded like a good idea until further down the page he mentioned his wife). A photograph showed a long-haired hippy in his 60s with a subtle, possibly wily face bending over a cooking pot on a camp fire: this one wanted a bisexual woman keen on astrology with whom to have a child. A lecturer in computer studies wrote a letter in which he portrayed himself as a boozy failure dismally conscious of his thin arms, and enclosed an out-of-focus snapshot of himself with his head cut off. An American professional who divided his time between Cambridge and Denmark gave me the horsepower and registration of his car and motorbike, and described himself discouragingly as *"very neat (obsessive/compulsive?) and fastidious"*.

Some were unintentionally funny. One was addressed: *"To a woman whose thoughts breathe spice and whose words burn into the pages of the mind"* - the writer described himself as *"a* director, muscular and fit, creative, handsome and gritty". Another introduced himself as "a tall, handsome, professional, male naturist, original and supportive. Varied interests, some to your personal advantage."

However, I gave the biscuit for suavity to the surgeon with substantial business connections, who wrote: "I am considered very attractive, 5'10 1/2" tall. I feel that our qualities will be complementary, as will our interests - mine are multifarious. I am genuine, sincere, loving, kind, caring, friendly, warm, with integrity and zest, intelligent, articulate, adventurous, fun-loving, affectionate, romantic, amorous, sensual, vibrant personality, charming, amusing, witty, great sense of humour." His exuberant handwriting filled the whole page and ended in a flurry of kisses. Every time I picked up this letter to reply to it I was lost for words.

Two of the writers seemed a little strange. One was the author of the illuminated manuscript the size of a tea towel. This was a quite beautiful piece of work and must have taken hours to complete. It took me a full hour to decipher, and turned out to be a bizarre rambling stream-of-consciousness in which the writer likened his build and character to that of a vulture.

The other was a poet (there were several poets). He sent me a booklet of verses that proclaimed his love for the ghost of a dead poetess, and were full of rustling leaves, tears, whisperings, moths, candle flames, swirling mist and bitter fruit. I wrote to thank him: it was painstakingly produced. His reply was a surprise. When he was not living in his imagination, he turned out to be a long-distance commuter, a munitions engineer with a wife and daughter.

I wrote back that I was only interested in single men, but he had me confused, somehow, with the dead poetess of his dreams, and began writing me poems full of faery swarms and glinting lanterns. One such was addressed to the spirit that lived inside my house: *"I felt your nearness stirring in the shadows"*; I realized with a shudder that he must have driven there and parked outside to have a good look at it, and possibly at me. A further firm letter from me elicited a *"Farewell to Melusina"*, and a promise that he would wait in exile, his tears freezing as they fell, until I summoned him to return. This man, though odd, was not to be feared, because it was not the real me that he was interested in, but a dream.

I put all the letters into piles, graded according to the response required, and found there were about ten men I thought I might like to meet. Among them was P, who wrote at length about himself, and amusingly. P had given up a successful career in computers to do an English degree; he was now a teacher; he had swum with the famous dolphin Freddie, and was involved with mentally handicapped children. I spoke to P on the phone and liked him, but he was desperately lonely and managed to convince himself within minutes that I was his only hope, which frightened me away.

Another interesting *Guardian* reader, who appealed to me because of his cheerful directness, was K, a disenchanted labourer who now spent most of his time working for charity. He wrote that he was just off to Romania with a truckload of relief supplies. He would send me a postcard when he got there, and maybe I could go with him on a future trip. He sounded friendly and refreshingly unworried about making an impression: I was sorry not to hear from him again.

Then there was C, a single father who grew his own vegetables, worked part-time in a library, made jewellery on the kitchen table and enjoyed junk shops. There were cat paw marks all over his letters (a plus point in my eyes). We corresponded for a while, but he seemed to me to be trying too hard and apologizing too much, and my enthusiasm ran out.

I was hoping to find somebody who was positive, with energy and confidence, though not above laughing at himself. Looks were important too - not colour of eyes or "all own hair", as some of the adverts depressingly put it, but liveliness and alertness of expression. And I wanted this man to be slim and reasonably fit, because being in good shape means that you respect your body and take care of it. All these attributes seemed to meet most happily in B, and I stared at his photograph for so long that I burned my porridge.

THE FIRST DATE

A first blind date is a terrifying prospect because unless you are very lucky, you will find it difficult to forget the unnaturalness of the situation. Here you are, two strangers who have met to put your cards on the table and find out in this quite clinical way whether you could generate between you the deepest of feelings. A clear view all the way up to the altar gives rise to unrealistic expectations, and at the same time leaves you feeling unprotected and defenceless.

Take heart. After the first date things get better, and the pressure to succeed fades as the idea suddenly blossoms that you are supposed to be doing this to enjoy yourself. You will surely have a memorable time, even if it's not memorable in quite the way you hoped.

B, the man who was so attractive that he made me burn my porridge, was my first date. We had got on well speaking together on the phone, but I was severely eaten up with nerves at the prospect of coming face to face. We were due to meet on New Year's Day. I spent the whole day in bed with a hangover, feeling very sick. It was lucky that B and I had decided we were compatible enough not to restrict ourselves to a half-hour meeting and to go for a Chinese meal: I kept my bowl hidden from his view behind the heated serving tray and ate one grain of rice at a time.

B was dressed expensively but with discreet good taste; he was perfectly groomed and his manners were easy and faultless. I imagined he could partner even the clumsiest of women round the dance floor and make her feel like a bird. He was probably the most eligible bachelor anyone could hope to meet. I felt hugely relieved when the evening was over. B and I lived in different worlds. I could not imagine him dishevelled with earth under his fingernails and paint on his clothes; when I told him I kept 47 chickens his interest was polite rather than enthusiastic.

However, the story of B was a success in its own way, because I introduced him to a friend of mine and they saw each other regularly for several months.

I met another man whom I saw only once: M. Our correspondence began very promisingly, but M's strategy, as he later admitted, was to be cheeky and amusing and to present all his best points, and then gradually to slip in the factors he felt would not go in his favour. Thus his second letter mentioned a teenage son living at home, the third hinted at a lodger, and his fourth touched briefly on a three-year-old daughter whom he looked after for half the week.

When M said he was a writer, I understood that he wrote for a living, but he meant that he was unemployed and spent a lot of time in the pub having socio-political conversation with a little group of intellectuals rather Brechtian in character. By the time I read the bit about the Brechtian intellectuals and some details of a recent holiday with the mother of his three-year-old child - who, incidentally, he said was rather upset that he should be answering Lonely Hearts ads - it was too late: I was sitting on a train that was just pulling out of the station on a seven-hour journey to M's home town.

M was rather sheepish when I put it to him that he had not been entirely honest with me, and that it was really not fair to present himself as single and free when he had so many commitments. Still, I couldn't help liking him, and feeling sorry that I had shattered his dream. He drew some money out of the building society and bought me a baked potato filled with coleslaw, and cheered up no end when I said I was getting the early train home. The next post brought a homegrown bulb of garlic from his garden as an atonement, but sadly I couldn't use it as it stank of tobacco.

There were two men whom I saw several times, T and H. The first time I met T, we had a very pleasant day at the seaside. I was relaxed because I had convinced myself in advance that I wouldn't like him, and therefore didn't have to worry about whether he liked me. I had spoken to him on the phone and he had the shrill public school voice that often announces crippling personality problems; he was a civil servant and very nervous. I should have listened to my instincts. T was clever and entertaining, and for a while we got on quite well, but then I stepped back and took another look at him and tuned in to the message behind the words he was saying and I liked him a great deal less; and the cooler I became, the more he clung. He did not seem to understand the word "no". Frankly, he turned into a pest, but in the end his energy ran out and he disappeared.

H was altogether more likeable. Affectionate and sentimental by nature, he worked with young people in the theatre, and put his whole self into his job. He had very little time to devote to a budding friendship, and I think he had unconsciously arranged it like this to protect himself from getting involved again, because although he claimed he had recovered, he was still suffering very badly from the breakup of his marriage a couple of years before. H and I both wanted to like each other, but after a while we had to admit the sparkle just was not there.

We parted with mutual regard, and there ended my adventures among the small ads. Although I did not meet anyone who would play an important part in my life, I did find the whole experience fascinating. I made contact with some very interesting men whom I would never have got to know in the normal course of things. I had two friendships that lasted several weeks. I saw quite a lot of the country I had not visited before, in the company of people who were pleased to show me round where they lived. Perhaps most heartening of all was the knowledge that there is a large network of single people out there, who live in isolated parts of the country or rarely get to meet anyone new through their work, or whose children tie them to home, and that whenever you're feeling sociable, you can plug into this network and make contact for the price of a stamp.

The price of a stamp put my correspondent B, a single mother, in touch with her second husband, a single father. She writes: *"We met through a newspaper ad. I answered 10; I very nearly answered nine, because the tenth didn't mention marriage. But then I wrote and met my husband, who is the most wonderful man on earth."*

THE "PROFESSIONAL" LONELY HEARTS ADVERTISER

There are some people who conduct their entire social life through the Lonely Hearts columns. One of the men I saw several times had married a woman he had met through an advertisement, and after their divorce three years later, had started to meet new girlfriends in the same way. He had been doing it solidly for years. There was nothing wrong in this, of course - except that I discovered he was still scouring the small ads for likely partners while we were going out together. It had become a compulsion, and decidedly off-putting it was too, because it seemed that he was still hoping the next post might bring a letter from somebody better.

This sort of person is a "collector" - someone to be avoided, because he is not really looking to focus on one person, and maybe incapable of doing so. Of course, "collectors" come in both sexes. Just as this book was going to press, I looked through the latest copy of Dateline's magazine and was surprised to see one of the ads Dateline had sent me months before, to show how their most popular ads were worded (see page 30). So here was a woman who had received around 150 replies, advertising again, and with exactly the same words.

Unless you recognize a collector from a previous advert, you may find him or her difficult to spot even when you come face to face, as happened with me. The reason is, of course, that your date is very practised at making convincingly smooth opening moves in a "test-tube relationship", because he or she has done it so many times before. As long as you remember to take things slowly, you won't get hurt, and you can hopefully make your exit without hurting the other person either - in the secure knowledge that they are in any case much more at ease in pursuit of a mate than they would be in settling down with one.

A True Story

This true story is short, but not sweet. It illustrates one of the worst fears of people who venture into the Lonely Hearts columns.

Andrew had answered an advert in *Time Out*, and had arranged to meet a woman for a drink. He was to go to the block of flats where she lived, then phone her from the box outside, and she would come down to meet him. He went to the flats, he found the phone box and dialled her number. *"I won't be long,"* said the woman, *"I'm just settling the baby down."*

Andrew was perplexed: the woman hadn't said anything about a baby. He walked across the street and stood where he could see the entrance to the block of flats, without being immediately visible himself. In a little while, a woman came out, pushing a doll's pram. She could hardly see over the top of the pram. Andrew panicked. He ran.

One can feel for both parties in this sad story. Dreadful mismatches like this must be rare, but could never happen through a reputable agency.

SOME THOUGHTS ON LETTER-WRITING

Meeting people through the personal columns requires a great deal of letter-writing, and this can be quite tiring - physically exhausting, if you're wielding a pen instead of tapping out your letter on a keyboard, and certainly mentally gruelling, if you're having to churn out tens of enthusiastic descriptions of your enchantingly vivacious personality. It's quite easy to become jaded and cynical about your own most attractive attributes, if you have to keep writing about them.

My advice is to think out a core description of yourself and to use this as the heart of each letter, varying the beginning and the end according to whom you are writing to. This means that your letters will always be fresh and personal - more enjoyable both to write and to receive.

Here are some other points:

● Be humorous, but don't go mad: you're trying to project yourself, not to disappear under a smokescreen of hilarious badinage.

● Always be honest. (This includes not lying about your age.) If you are dishonest (like M was, above), you will always be found out and the friendship will be over before it has begun. Be honest to do yourself justice, as well as out of consideration for the other person. Accept yourself and be comfortable with yourself. Remember that you're looking for someone who suits you as you really are, not as you think you should be.

● It's perfectly acceptable to type a letter or to use a wordprocessor, as long as you keep it personal. But don't fall into officialese, as did one of my correspondents, who wrote: *"Dear Lady, your advert in* The Times *has been brought to my attention. Could you please communicate with me in order to arrange for a meeting at a place and time convenient to yourself."*

● Don't ever send out photocopied letters. I had several of these and I'm afraid I didn't answer one. Feeling that you are just a random target in a mass-leafleting campaign does not endear you to the sender.

● Don't enclose anything that you want returned. Some people photocopy photographs of themselves, but it's better to get mini-prints made, see page 174.

● Answer as many letters as you can, and as tactfully as you can. It is very cheering to get a pleasant letter from a stranger, even if it's just to say thank you, sorry and good luck.

● Keep letters to about one page in length.

● When you're answering other people's ads, the same guidelines for writing letters apply. You may prefer to give only your phone number and no address, and you may decide to keep the personal details pretty vague - just in case you turn out to be answering the ad of someone you know!

For all the excitement it generates, this method of contacting people is likely to be pretty random. Don't be disappointed, therefore, if what seems like sackfuls of mail yield very few men you really want to meet. From my own experience, I would say about one in ten sounded promising. Advertising requires stamina, and there may be times when you feel discouraged, especially if a kind friend keeps asking you: *"Well, have you met him yet?"* Treat the whole business as lightheartedly as you can, enjoy the novelty, and you may strike lucky.

Chapter Three

FOR EVER AND EVER - MARRIAGE BUREAUX

KATHARINE ALLEN

Just behind London's Oxford Street is the Katharine Allen marriage bureau, run by Mrs Penrose Halson and her husband Bill, from a charming flat full of antiques that doubles as her office. It is comfortable, there are interesting things to look at, and Mrs Halson's engaging manner dispels any remaining apprehension her potential client might be feeling. Being invited to sit in an armchair by the fire in the front room, or even more cosily in the snug little room at the back with its original cast-iron range and copper kettle, makes the visitor feel privileged and trusted: a good start to the hour-long interview that helps both parties decide if joining the bureau is going to be the right move for you.

The bureau was established in 1960 by Katharine Allen, and Penrose Halson was a former client, though she didn't meet Mr Halson through the bureau, but when he came to rent her spare room. (Renting out a room is something she wholeheartedly advises her clients to try!) Her bureau is a member of the Society of Marriage Bureaux, whose code of practice protects clients against financial collapse. This is clearly a most important consideration, especially in the light of what happened when the most expensive of all bureaux, Helena International, went bust. Helena charged £2,000 plus VAT for a service that included personality testing and advice about clothes and make-up, ran medical and criminal checks on all its members, and promised a match that would bring wealth and status. Its demise left hundreds of middle-aged women distraught; many with no savings.

As Mrs Halson is quick to point out, people who use the services of a marriage bureau do not generally want to publicize the fact by complaining about unfair treatment, and unscrupulous operators can take advantage of this. Unfortunately, the Society of Marriage Bureaux now has only one member, and that is Katharine Allen. Mrs Halson has approached other bureaux and asked them to join, but no other satisfies the criteria for membership, which are that clients must be legally free to marry (other bureaux accept separated people) and must be interviewed in person.

The hallmark of Katharine Allen is its personal service. Mrs Halson does not use a computer, preferring to trust her instinct and her experience in building up a picture of her clients and their requirements. There is a questionnaire for you to fill in, but it is refreshingly basic, dealing with height, weight, profession etc. and not calling upon your talent for describing your personality. This is left to Mrs Halson, and during the initial interview, for which she charges a nominal fee, she jots down some impressions.

If you both agree that the bureau has

something to offer you - and in only one case has there ever been a disagreement over this - a registration fee is payable that entitles you to membership for a year. Subsequent years of membership cost considerably less, and a further fee is payable if you marry through the bureau. Members supply a photograph, but this is for office reference only. Mrs Halson does not send out photographs to prospective partners, for two reasons. The first is that photographs often do little justice to their subjects, and she would prefer members not to judge or be judged by them; the second is to protect privacy and confidentiality. She finds that her clients do not like the idea of having their photographs pored over by complete strangers, and this is especially true of clients who are in the public eye.

When Mrs Halson finds someone she thinks it would be worth your while to meet, she writes to the woman first, because she finds that her clients prefer it this way, and gives her a few brief details of the man - his name, profession, height etc. She will supply some additional information on request, but does not give emotive descriptions of character, as personal impressions are always subjective and no one can predict sexual chemistry.

If the woman reacts favourably, she then writes to the man with *her* details, including address and phone number if she wishes. It is up to the man to get in touch. *"And this is where there is sometimes a problem,"* said Mrs Halson, shaking her head in exasperation. The men on her books are often in such high-powered jobs that they have little time to invest in searching for a partner, which is of course the reason why they joined in the first place. Their delay in responding, especially if the answer is eventually negative, can be very demoralizing for the woman waiting at the other end, and Mrs Halson asks women to tell her when men don't get in touch, so that she can coax them gently into action. This part of her job demands all her tact and patience. She must not nag, or that will put her men off altogether, and she must be utterly discreet, which means never leaving messages with secretaries or housekeepers or even on private answering machines, in case they are heard by mistake by a third party.

As in most agencies and bureaux, Katharine Allen has a shortage of men and a preponderance of women over 40, which is another reason why Mrs Halson approaches the women first with the men's details, and not the other way around. There are around 1,000 people on her books, mainly professionals of graduate level or similar, from different parts of the country, and aged, at the time of writing, from 23 to 88.

Because choosing a marriage partner is a highly selective business, people who join Katharine Allen can expect fewer introductions in a year than they would get from an introduction agency, and some clients remain on the books for several years. One man was with the Heather Jenner bureau, a victim of the recession taken over by Katharine Allen, for 24 years until his persistence paid off.

Persistence and patience are important if you want to succeed in finding a spouse, says

Mrs Halson. Her clients can help their own chances improve by keeping in touch with her and letting her know their reactions to each introduction: that way she builds up a better idea of what sort of person would suit them. Sometimes she is surprised by her own success. Recently, she "married" a 56-year-old woman who had been on the books for six years. This woman was tall and extremely intelligent, which, in combination with her age, made her difficult to introduce to more than a couple of men a year. Then one day, a man walked into the bureau whom Mrs Halson recognized immediately as her perfect match. Her first idea was to introduce this man to one or two other women on the books, and then to put him in touch with the "right" one; she thought this would make it seem all the more "right", but in the end she dared not risk his falling for one of the others. She brought them together straight away, and the tall intelligent woman received her reward for all the useful feedback she had given to the bureau over the years.

What other advice did Mrs Halson have for

her members, apart from keeping in touch and never giving up? First, she recommended that though the search for a spouse is a serious business, it should be approached in a light-hearted manner. Members are very often anxious and apprehensive before their first date, but the occasion is invariably much pleasanter than they feared. When you meet the other person, she says, it is important not to come too quickly to a judgment. Especially, do not feel that because you are not in love within the first half-hour, all is lost. Chemical reactions often do not take place instantly, but grow out of better knowledge of each other. The important thing to establish at a first meeting is whether you enjoyed yourself in the other person's company. Mrs Halson encourages her members to drop each other a friendly card suggesting a further meeting, if that is what they would like. The answer might be negative, and a negative is never easy to give or to receive over the phone, much less in person.

Though marriage is what her clients are

looking for, Mrs Halson says that they find many other benefits on the way. People make friends and introduce each other to more friends; they find jobs for each other and for each other's children. Meeting new people and expanding your social circle boosts confidence and self-esteem, never more so than for the widow or widower who has had no new one-to-one contact for perhaps 30 years. And one unusual side-effect was acknowledged by a young man who has not yet found a partner, but who is enjoying the search: it has made him more tolerant.

As I mentioned previously, most people's social circles get smaller as they grow older, and this is of course why people need a service like that offered at Katharine Allen. Mrs Penrose Halson believes that joining her bureau is only one of the ways in which her clients should seek to reverse the trend, and encourages them to get to meet more people through all sorts of other avenues, according to their personalities and interests. She points out that the more people you meet, the better chance you stand of meeting the one person you want to stay with.

MARRIAGE ASIAN-STYLE THROUGH WESTERN BUREAUX

In the Indian sub-continent, the selection of a marriage partner is by tradition a matter that concerns not just the individuals involved. As children come of age, large numbers of near and distant relatives look out for suitable candidates among their acquaintances. In the 1960s, with the influx of Asians into Britain, the network of extended families was stretched beyond practical usefulness, and the efficient introductions service that it provided was lost. British Asians have not established such large families because priorities in the West are different, they have easier access to contraception and are often subject to restrictions of finance and space. A man or woman hoping to marry another British Asian will get fewer introductions because there are fewer people looking out for partners for their relatives. Arranged marriages made over a distance of thousands of miles stand less chance of success and some bring only misery, as in the two cases outlined below.

P was flown out to India by her parents to marry against her will. For an Asian woman this is an intolerable situation, because she has been brought up to believe that to disobey her parents is an extremely serious offence and will ruin the reputation of her family. P was thus faced with unhappiness whether she followed her instincts, or the call of duty.

S wrote to tell me that shortly after his wife arrived from India she left him, saying that she had only agreed to their arranged marriage in order to start a new independent life for herself in the West.

In the absence of a large number of relatives to perform introductions, young Asians are turning to professional agencies for help, and this way of meeting potential partners is proving an ideal marriage of Asian traditions and Western techniques.

THE SUMAN MARRIAGE BUREAU

This bureau is based in Southall in west London. It was Europe's first such bureau for Asians, and today it is the biggest Asian bureau in the world. It is also a founder member of the Association of British Introduction Agencies. Your year's membership fee (see page 174 for details) entitles you to an unlimited number of introductions to people who meet your requirements, whether of height, age, religion or sub-caste. Details of background, such as your ancestral village, are important factors in choosing a partner, explains Ramesh Bhargava, who runs the bureau with his wife Suman. Because the sub-continent is so vast and its customs and traditions so varied, it is important to ensure that potential partners speak the same language and the same dialect, and eat the same type of food.

Despite its size, the Suman bureau interviews each client personally, along with his or her family, if that is preferred. It also offers its premises for meetings between the people it introduces, and again, their families are welcome to go along. *"Keeping your family involved in what you do is natural,"* says A, a British-educated Asian who married through the bureau. *"I love and respect my parents, and whoever I was going to marry had to get to know them and get on with them."*

Suman has over 4,000 Asian marriages to its credit, and has recently opened a new category in its files: for partnerships between white British males and Asian women. *"The men are looking for faithful wives and stability in marriage,"* says Ramesh Bhargava, *"and the women are searching for a more liberated lifestyle. That means avoiding domineering Asian men, dowry problems and interfering in-laws. Asian husbands* are *more domineering. They expect their wives to do all the work at home even if they have a full-time job outside. A Briton will share housework, and he and his wife will relax together."*

THE ASIAN MARRIAGE AND FRIENDSHIP BUREAU INTERNATIONAL

This bureau is also a member of the ABIA. Some of its literature is worded in a strikingly similar way to that of the older established Suman bureau, above. Its fees are comparable (see page 174), but its operation is more like that of Dateline. AMFBI uses a computer to set up introductions and does not interview its clients personally. Its questionnaire is less wide-ranging than Dateline's, but it does ask, amongst other things, which of 19 languages you speak; whether you wear glasses or contact lenses always, sometimes or never; whether you drink, smoke, or eat meat; what sort of hair you have (anything from "none" to "permed"); and whether you drive or own a car. You tick another similar set of boxes to describe the partner you want. Without having asked any questions about personality, the brochure then declares: *"We have now got a detailed and complete picture of the sort of person you are and the type of person you are looking for."*

Once your details are matched up with those of the others on the computer, you are sent names, addresses and phone numbers, and where possible, photographs. The bureau has variations on this service, the most expensive being active membership that lasts until you find a partner. There is also an advertising service, whereby the bureau will place your ad in a suitable publication in any part of the world. It will also translate your ad for you into any of 19 languages (presumably a service for people who want to meet partners they won't be able to talk to or understand).

Chapter Four

INTRODUCING MR RIGHT - AGENCIES

Agencies come and go, and some within a very short space of time, taking all your hopes and your savings with them. So the first essential is to check that the agency you are thinking of joining is an established business with a proven track record and not a fly-by-night operation that hides behind a box number or a telephone number only.

The best protection you can get is to pick an agency that belongs to the Association of British Introduction Agencies (ABIA), which drew up a code of practice on the instigation of the Office of Fair Trading when it was formed in 1981. The ABIA has an arbitration service that can help clients with complaints against member companies, but until its code of practice is made law, and introduction agencies are allowed to operate only with a government licence, the association cannot help clients who have been cheated by non-members. All the agencies in this book are members of the ABIA, except Katharine Allen, which is sole member of a similar organization, the Society of Marriage Bureaux.

The next thing to consider is the type of service you require. The cheapest is usually a listings service: details of new members are added to a register, and you receive a list of all members, or those in a group you have selected on joining, and at intervals throughout your membership. Contact is made in most cases by letter via the bureau.

If you choose a computer dating service (see page 133), your details are fed into a computer that assesses compatibility. You are sent names, addresses and phone numbers of a selection of people, but no further information about them.

The most personalized service comes from agencies where the principal or members of staff work on the cases of individual clients. Within this category you will find agencies that select partners for you and send you first names and phone numbers without telling you why they have made the choice; agencies that provide you with a great deal of detail; and other agencies that let you choose yourself from a stack of personal profiles and photographs. Some of these agencies place great importance on getting to know their clients personally, while others never get to meet them.

Of course price is an important consideration, and membership fees for the time of writing are given together with addresses and telephone numbers on page 174. Some of the agencies are very expensive, but you may feel that this guarantees the seriousness of their clients, or you may decide to go for a similar service that costs less. Often the listings agencies offer really good value for money. If the agency of your choice is too expensive for your pocket, it's always worth asking for a reduction. Several bureaux will consider discounts for the unemployed.

Area is another factor: some agencies are

nationwide, some are regional, and others are only really practical for those who live in or around London. There are three bureaux in the ABIA that cater specifically for those in remote country areas, so there should be something in this book for everyone in England, Scotland and Wales.

Make an initial selection of two or three agencies after reading this chapter, then ring up and ask them to send you details. You should be able to tell a lot about the agency from the way the staff speak to you on the phone. In order to get the best out of the service they provide, you must get on well with them, because the better they get to know you, the better idea they will have of the type of person you would like to meet. Ask them whether they have social events, if that is what you would like, and ask too, if they'd be prepared to take you off the books temporarily when you meet someone. This takes off the pressure and gives you valuable extra time because your membership is not ticking away while you are getting to know someone who may turn out to be unsuitable.

From the information the agency sends you, you should be able to tell if you will like its members. There are agencies for all sorts of people, from green to glamorous, so choose the one whose image you feel most comfortable with.

If you go for an interview, wear clothes you feel good in, not those you'd wear for a job interview. Remember that the interview is two-way: it's not just the principal assessing whether she or he would like you as a member, it's also you assessing the principal and everything about the agency: its staff, the atmosphere in the office, and above all, the type of person it has on its books. You are the one with the money, and there are other choices open to you. Ask how many members they have of the opposite sex and in your preferred age group, and ask whether they are likely to be able to find you a partner or not. A good agency will give you an honest answer without making you feel rejected. Do not be disappointed if you are advised not to join: it does not mean that you are unacceptable or unloveable, merely that you are looking in the wrong place. Try a different kind of bureau, or try advertising.

Once you've found and joined an agency that you like, work with it by giving the staff feedback. Tell them if you don't get enough introductions, and tell them how you feel about the people you meet; if it doesn't seem to be working after a while, discuss changing your profile or your specifications.

Don't expect miracles. The agency can do no more than attempt to put you in touch with other members, and this is in itself no guarantee that all of them will want to meet you. Be realistic and persevere: every introduction is a gamble, and the best ones are just as likely to be made in the last months of your membership as in the first, because new members are joining all the time.

Lastly, enjoy the quest, and be prepared for some surprises. Unpromising first meetings often lead to better things, and you may meet some good friends on the way.

ANGLIA FRIENDSHIP BUREAU

This agency concentrates, as you would expect, on East Anglia and surrounding counties, but welcomes members nationwide. An initial enquiry to this bureau elicits very little information, not even the name of the proprietor. However, Anglia Friendship Bureau is a member of the Association of British Introduction Agencies and has been operating successfully since 1975, so perhaps these two facts should be recommendation enough to someone who lives in the area and is looking for a discreet, no frills and reasonably-priced service (see page 174).

Prospective members are asked to fill in a brief questionnaire, and may call at the bureau by appointment if they wish. Within ten days of joining, members are provided with three or four introductions, comprising first names, telephone numbers and brief details of their matches. Further sets of introductions are supplied for a minimal extra fee.

The agency seems unexcited by its own

success: *"On occasion we do have wedding cake and invitations presented to us. Many members request that their details be removed from the register when they find a partner. We feel a sense of satisfaction in knowing that we have helped in bringing many happy couples together."*

CONNECTIONS

This is the only personal introductions service in the East Midlands registered with the ABIA. It is run by Diana Ballantyne, who promises hundreds of discerning members from a wide range of professional and clerical backgrounds. Her literature is somewhat out-of-date, as it refers to a choice of register, but it appears that her standard register has been closed, leaving the more expensive professional and executive register as the client's only option.

All clients are interviewed, though when during the enrolment procedure the interview takes place is not made clear. Prospective clients should make sure they have the chance to meet the principal before they decide to part with any money. Ms Ballantyne offers to interview you at your own home if you wish for a separate fee. This would cover an hour-long consultation and advise on filling out the registration form, should you need it. The form is in fact quite simple, with lists of personal characteristics and leisure interests - cross out those that don't apply to you. You are also asked to specify the type of car you drive, the salary range that applies to you, and your preferred style of dress (formal /smart /trendy /fashionable /casual /ethnic /own individual style /traditional). Connections promises to introduce you to at least 20 people within your year's membership, or you will be offered a further year's membership free of charge. No computer is used in the selection procedure. Once you have become a member, the principal looks through her files to find you a match, bearing in mind that you may be wishing to meet a friend of either sex or a potential partner. Once she has found someone she thinks will suit you, she writes describing the person and giving their first name only. If you like what you read, she then writes to him or her with similar details and gives out phone numbers. You are then free to contact each other. A letter with a stamped addressed envelope will secure you another introduction as soon as you like.

COUNTRY PARTNERS

This is run from a cottage in Herefordshire by Heather Heber Percy, who understands isolation, having lived for 15 years on a remote Mediterranean island with only her two children and some chickens for company. She set up her agency in 1985, intending to unite people living in isolated country areas of Britain, but soon had requests from people feeling isolated in towns as well. This is not a cheap service (see page 174), but Heather does offer each client an interview with someone in their area, during the evening or at a weekend if necessary, and hopes to provide a couple of introductions a month. If you find the fee too high, you can discuss a reduction in confidence with your interviewer. Heather will not accept anyone she feels she will be unable to put in touch with compatible prospective partners.

The first step is to fill in a questionnaire that includes car registration number (with safety in mind), and spaces for you to give a brief description of your appearance and character and that of the sort of person you would like to meet. The next step is to arrange for an interview. Then, when you have agreed to join, details of your first contact are put in the post to you, and simultaneously yours are put in the post to him or her. The bureau would like to hear from you each time you meet a new person, as your reactions help them to build up a picture of your character and your requirements.

DISDATE

See Handidate.

DRAWING DOWN THE MOON

Mary Balfour runs what is probably Britain's best-known introduction agency, Drawing Down the Moon. The name comes from Greek mythology, in which to draw down the moon was a potent love charm. This agency's service is upmarket, personalized, sophisticated and, at the time of writing, the most expensive in the ABIA (see page 174). However, the high price does not deter suitable members; in fact for some it acts as a sort of guarantee that everyone who joins "means business". And business is brisk, despite the recession: Mary reckons to send out around 40,000 personal profiles a year, which means 40,000 potential introductions. She can't tell you her success rate, because very few people let her know when they finally meet their match.

Drawing Down the Moon was established in 1984 and used to be run from a bookshop near the British Museum. In 1986 Mary Balfour, a former model and sociology graduate, who had spent 12 months researching the market in introduction agencies for an opening, gave up her job as head of an adult education centre, bought Drawing Down the Moon and moved it to Kensington High Street. The system she inherited was so chaotic that during the first couple of months she succeeded in introducing one woman to her own brother and one man to himself; now, with a staff of eight, the service is fully streamlined.

Prospective members are sent the agency's details, and if they like what they see, they are invited in for an informal interview. Mary says that most of her clients are positive, confident, and clear about the sort of person and the sort of relationshp they are looking for. If you fit the bill, which means that you are a professional in the business, creative or academic world, a graduate or similar, and live in London or within easy commuting distance, and are under 40 if you are a woman, then you will probably be invited to join.

The next step is to complete your questionnaire, which gives plenty of space for self-expression and even asks who or what you would like to be if you were not yourself. (Did you know Margaret Thatcher would like to be Mother Theresa, and the Princess Royal a truck driver?) This done, you look through the files of the opposite sex, reading their profiles and examining their photographs, and select eight or ten people you would like to meet. This is a fascinating exercise that could easily take all day, but Mary knows all her clients and has a remarkably good memory, and can save everyone time by quickly guiding you to the ones who might appeal.

Your profiles are sent out to each one of your selections, and it is up to them to get in touch with you, usually by phone, though of course they could write via the agency. Your own details go on file, and in this way people can select you. You are encouraged to go into the office and make a fresh selection every six to eight weeks, or as often as you like. Mary feels satisfied if you meet one-third of the people they contact on your behalf; for a lucky few, like the woman who was chosen by 172 different men, the problem is too much choice.

The agency also offers the chance to attend regular social gatherings at a local wine bar. Members wear name tags: if you speak to, or even catch sight of someone you like the look of, you can ring the office the next day and ask for your profile to be sent to that person, if you were too reticent to show your interest.

Beth met her husband Tim through Drawing Down the Moon. She had a very good social life and was surrounded by men in her job, but the men she went out with were either confirmed bachelors or divorced and definitely not looking for another commitment. She chose Drawing Down the Moon because: *"It seemed discreet and sensible, and the high membership fee guarantees no messing about."* She was not disappointed. *"My first dates were always nerve-wracking, but they ended up being amusing and easy because at least no one was looking, as they always are when people try to match you up at dinner parties."* She met Tim after three months. *"I thought he was great fun, but soon after we met I had to go away, so I asked Drawing Down the Moon to put me on hold. When I told them I was going to the south of France, they said they had a member down there I could meet! I came back and contacted Tim again, and we took it very gently from there.* "Beth is 38: she admitted lying about her age by a couple of years. *"Tim was very amused when he found out, because he had lied about his height by half an inch!"*

Richard has fallen in love with a woman he met through Drawing Down the Moon. He is 35 and self-employed in a one-man business, but his positive attitude would not let him remain in isolation: *"People should do something about their lives,"* he says, *"take the knocks instead of sitting moping at home."* He joined Drawing Down the Moon because he was impressed by its publicity and recommended by a friend. After a relationship that lasted a year, he rejoined, and within three weeks he met Sally. I wondered if this was not a bit soon after the end of his previous relationship. *"I feel very ready for it psychologically,"* said Richard, *"and I've met someone who is at the same stage of personal development as myself."*

The Farmers And Country Bureau

This is a nationwide service with connections abroad, run by a farmer's wife from a 300-acre sheep and dairy farm in Derbyshire. Patricia Warren set up her agency in 1982 for people who live and work in the countryside, though she also has members who are town dwellers and would like to find a partner and a new life in the village or on a farm. The bureau offers a valuable service to those who are isolated by geography and want to share the beauty of their surroundings, and especially to those working in agriculture who are tied to the farm and find it difficult to get away to meet people. The books are open to anyone, and include landed gentry, those with degrees in agriculture, and farm labourers.

Prospective clients complete a questionnaire and send in a photograph (for office use only) and a small registration fee. A larger fee (see page 174) is payable on accepting your first introduction, after which no further fee is payable. You are entitled to up to seven introductions, and these may come over one year or over several years, according to availability of compatible people. The bureau has a large number of women over 45, so they stand less chance of success, while men in this age range have a wide selection of prospective partners. Members generally do not visit the bureau, because not everyone finds it easy to get to Derbyshire, but an interview can be arranged for a fee if you wish.

When Patricia Warren and her staff find you someone they think will be compatible, they write and tell you about the person. You should reply within five days, saying whether you would like to meet. The other person is then contacted, and once both parties have agreed to a meeting, names, addresses and possibly phone numbers are released. The bureau does not expect anyone to meet a stranger, and recommends that you get to know each other through letters or phone calls before arranging to meet, especially if you live at some distance from each other. Obviously, the more flexible you can be about moving home with this bureau, the better chance you stand of finding a mate.

Pat says: *"It's unusual if we don't have two weddings a month."* She has many successful matches to her credit, including twin nurses who had a double wedding to country bridegrooms, and a village postmistress who went to the Falklands to marry a sheep farmer.

THE FRIENDSHIP BUREAU

This agency covers Devon and Cornwall and has been operating since 1974. Its clients are any age from 17 to 80+, and come from all walks of life. The principal, Jayne Spencer, offers two types of service on receipt of a reasonable fee (see page 174) and your answers filled in on her short questionnaire. The cheaper self-selection service entitles you to receive a list of the bureau's members in your requested age group - everyone is asked to write a short description of themselves and say if they want a box number or their telephone number to appear with it. Your own entry will appear on the latest list so that members are free to contact you as you are them. Updated lists are sent out each month for the year of your subscription. The more expensive service offers, as well as the list, up to four contacts hand-picked by Jayne Spencer, who obviously has access to more details about her clients than those which appear on the list. Further hand-picked selections can be ordered throughout the year for no extra cost.

Jayne Spencer has a thick file of thankyou letters from satisfied clients, and sent me one of her success stories: of Peggy and George, now in their late sixties. Both had been widowed and were looking for nothing more than companionship when they joined the bureau. Peggy was given George's name straight away. Feeling a great deal of trepidation, she rang him up: they got on very well and spoke every day for a week. After another seven days, George suggested Peggy should get a train to his home town. When she arrived at the station her terror returned, and she thought how ridiculous it was for a woman of her age to be going on a blind date, but as soon as she got into the taxi beside George, she knew everything would be alright: *"He saw how nervous I was and simply put a big comforting hand over mine. From that moment I felt completely safe and happy."*

The following Friday, the visit was repeated and over a cup of tea at George's house: *"He simply looked at me and said: 'Will you marry me?' I was so taken aback, I said: 'I beg your pardon?' For heaven's sake, we hadn't even kissed! But he said to me: 'Peggy, I just know we will be happy.'"*

Just five weeks later, with the support of both their families, they were married, and four years on Peggy says: *"We still thank God every day for this new beginning, and for such happiness."*

FRIENDSHIPS

This is run by Jennifer Stacey in Pontefract

and covers the north of England, concentrating mainly on Yorkshire and Humberside. It welcomes anyone over the age of 18, and is one of the few bureaux apart from those that cater especially for the disabled (see page 97) that specifically welcomes disabled members. Friendships also has links with Gingerbread, the organization concerned with one-parent families.

As a single parent herself, Jennifer is particularly aware that many divorced women are tied to their home and children, while divorced men often have more spare time and spare cash, and are willing to go out and spend it. As a result, she says she has more men on her books than women - which is unusual among the agencies I have spoken to. However, more of her men are interested in a lively social life rather than in commitment, and more of her women are interested in settling down with one person than painting the town red. So the men tend to see a number of women and the women tend to see fewer of the men.

The very low membership fee (see page

174) means that this bureau does not send out a glossy brochure, and neither is Jennifer Stacey able to select individual contacts, or contacts within a specific area or age group. What she does on receipt of your completed questionnaire and your cheque is add your name and details to her register, which is circulated monthly to all members. Some members give their phone numbers, so can be contacted direct, while others prefer to use a box number, and these may be contacted in writing via the agency.

Jennifer Stacey is down-to-earth and approachable, and welcomes telephone contact and feedback from her clients. Since she was divorced 12 years ago she has used adverts in the local press to meet people herself several times (it would be against her professional ethics to use her own agency). Once a colleague at a college where she worked answered one of her advertisements. She could not reply for fear of embarrassing him, but always after that felt very strange sitting opposite him in meetings.

HAND IN HAND

This is an introduction agency based in Dunstable that has nationwide coverage, but concentrates particularly on middle England. It sends out a fairly comprehensive questionnaire to its prospective clients. Complete this and return it with your membership fee (see page 174), and within one week you will be sent the first names (not surnames) and telephone numbers of three people to whom the agency would like to introduce you, along with their details. Where possible, the agency gives out names of people in your area, but it considers compatibility more important than distance. Up to 18 introductions are allowed a year. Your contacts will simultaneously receive details of you. The agency's literature says: *"It is customary for the gentleman to contact the lady in the first instance, but if you have heard nothing within five or six days it is perfectly acceptable to telephone him, or you may write to him via Head Office."*

Hand in Hand does not use a computer to

match its clients, but neither does it conduct personal interviews *"unless someone has not found a partner within a reasonable time or after a number of introductions"*. Its leaflet goes on: *"Head Office would like to get to the root of the problem in the unlikely event of this happening."* Personally, if I did not meet the man of my dreams within a "reasonable" length of time, I would keep quiet about it. I certainly would not be able to face being hauled into Head Office to have the root of my "problem" exposed.

I wrote to Hand in Hand for their information pack, and in reply I received a badly faded photocopy of a handwritten note that began: *"May I say how pleasant it was speaking to you the other day"* - not perhaps the best first impression for an agency that prides itself on personal service.

HANDIDATE AND DISDATE

These are two agencies especially for disabled

people, and they both offer a very valuable service. Disdate was established in 1981 by Bruce S. Brown, who is himself disabled. He found that his disability made it very difficult for him to make genuine friends, so he started the agency knowing what loneliness is, and determined to help himself and other people to overcome it. He says that the majority of people regard the disabled as a *"separate breed"*, but disabled people need normal relationships just like anyone else. People without a handicap are also welcome to join. Bruce charges a very small fee, and will provide you with three introductions based on a short questionnaire, in which you give some basic details about yourself and say whether you would prefer to be put in touch with someone for visiting, writing or telephoning. His is a non-profit-making organization, and the charge is made merely to cover expenses.

Handidate was devised and is run by Conrad Packwood, who was born with cerebral palsy. When he came to terms with his disability and was ready to meet other people of his own age, he approached an established agency but was told that it could not cater for his "special needs", which were of course no different from anyone else's special needs for friendship and love. He decided then and there to start his own agency. It was founded in 1987 and launched nationwide by BBCTV, since when it has brought together all sorts of people for love and friendship.

Handidate caters for people with any sort of disability, including multiple sclerosis, heart trouble, spina bifida, epilepsy, injuries from accidents, sensory impairment and cerebral palsy. It has members of every educational standard, from those with learning difficulties or no qualifications to those with diplomas and degrees. It has people who are unemployed, professional people, and people from every part of the social spectrum. It also caters for caring, understanding people without a disability.

The membership fee is low, and Conrad hopes to offer four introductions over one year. If he fails to find four suitable people within your area, you remain on the books for a further year free of charge. The questionnaire is excellent, and the literature includes recommendations from satisfied members that are a moving testimony to this agency's success.

HEDI FISHER INTRODUCTIONS

This is a founder member of the Association of British Introduction Agencies, and has 20 years' experience of matchmaking. Clients fill in a simple form, attaching a photograph for office use only, and are invited for an interview. Although Hedi Fisher is London-based, it operates across the country, and you don't need to come to London for an interview.

Hedi Fisher does not accept all prospective members. *"We enrol people in the professional and business world, with high standards, often with busy and demanding lives. We do our best to ensure that our members are attractive, reliable and well adjusted,"* says the agency's literature.

In Mrs Fisher's experience, most of her

members do not tell other people how they met their partner. Forty-year-old Yvonne has told only her mother and her sister that she met her husband Andrew through an introduction agency. *"It's nothing to be ashamed of,"* she says, *"but I feel it's nobody's business but ours."* Yvonne was apprehensive when she first joined Hedi Fisher: *"I was very nervous about the first couple of dates. I worried that it might be a totally unnatural and embarrassing experience with an 'arranged' feel, and the men looking me over as a potential bride."*

In fact once she was on her first date she quickly forgot how she had met the man she was with. *"The men tended to be more shy than me - and just as relieved at how painless it all was."* For Yvonne and Andrew it was not love at first sight, and in fact their first meeting was low-key and unpromising. *"He got his train home and I remember thinking, 'Well, that's that. I won't be hearing from him again.'"* But she did, and the relationship grew from the first weekend they spent together *"like any relationship, and after a while it becomes irrelevant how you meet."*

Janus Introduction Bureau

This is a nationwide agency. The name was chosen because Janus is the god of new beginnings: he stands poised on the threshold of change and looks back over experience and forward with hope. Janus has many offices all over the country (look in the press or your Yellow Pages for details), and advertises widely. Members are not interviewed personally, but despite its size, this is a service where all introductions are hand-picked.

Prospective members fill in a short questionnaire, which in addition to basic details like height, weight etc. also asks you to circle any of a list of adjectives that you feel describes your character. Among these are "passive" and "dominant": surely circling either would be more likely to repel than attract?

One good point that does distinguish this questionnaire from others is that it asks, in a confidential section for office reference only, whether your ultimate hope is to marry; to find a relationship that probably excludes marriage, for whatever reason; or to meet a variety of people, in order to provide an insight into alternative lifestyles, or to assist a process of personal readjustment, or merely for friendship. You can tick one or two of these options. Honesty here may well save misunderstandings and disappointments in meeting other Janus members. While some agencies try to exclude people on the rebound from a broken relationship, there is no doubt that many who join them do so in the hope of filling a gap in their lives and making themselves feel attractive and wanted again. Often, meeting people who have had a similar experience can restore confidence and help you to understand and accept your own grief.

Once Janus has received your completed questionnaire and membership fee, it sends out the non-confidential part of your questionnaire to selected members in your area, and you receive theirs. Your name, address and/or telephone number may be withheld from this information if you wish. Though total confidentiality does make the process more long-winded, some members have professional relationships with members of the public, such as doctors and dentists, and do not like to reveal their identity in the initial stages as it could cause embarrassment to both parties if they were matched with one of their patients. *"To the best of our knowledge,"* says Janus, *"we have never occasioned a single embarrassing incident."*

When you need more introductions, all you have to do is to send the bureau a stamped self-addressed envelope. Janus hopes to provide a minimum of eight introductions a year, and in many cases the number will be much greater, according to the availability of suitable people.

KENT INTRODUCTION SERVICE

This is a small personal agency run by Ann Baker and Roy Gilbert, both of whom have grown-up children and are divorced from their previous partners. Ann and Roy work from their home in Tonbridge, and they interview all their members themselves, usually in members' own homes. Talking to people in their own environment gives them an added insight into personality, tastes and lifestyle, and they believe their success rate is high. They are always available to talk to members on the phone and do not charge for this service; their fees are very reasonable. They put out a simple questionnaire and ask for a recent photograph, but will take one themselves at no extra cost to you, should you not have one. The photograph and questionnaire are for their reference files only: the matchmaking process is carried out by instinct and not by computer.

Ann and Roy do have hundreds of people of all ages and from all walks of life across Kent on their books, but rather than provide you with an introduction just for the sake of it, they prefer to wait, if necessary, until they feel they have a compatible match. They then send each party the first name, telephone number and home town of their opposite number, and await results. Clients are encouraged to keep in touch, as the more Roy and Ann know about you and the sort of person you are looking for, the better able they are to help.

Natural Friends

This was established in 1985 by Barbara Bradshaw in Culford near Bury St Edmunds, Suffolk, and now has well over 1,000 members nationwide. This is a very reasonably priced listings service for people who are interested in any aspect of green living. Only two or three of its large membership have admitted to being smokers, which is not surprising, as Natural Friends are keen on alternative therapies and holistic philosophies, personal development, astrology, herbalism, conservation, organic farming and gardening, natural history, the creative arts and crafts, rambling and youth hostelling, naturism, animal and human rights, world peace and health. Members are over 18, and some are over 80; there is a good balance between the sexes.

Prospective members write a description of

themselves and their interests, and on receipt of this and their membership fee, Barbara sends them a starter pack: you can choose 200 male advertisements, 200 female advertisements, or one set of at least 200 members of both sexes aged 50+. Further starter packs may be purchased separately: at the time of writing there are three for each sex. Your own profile will appear in the next update, and for a further small fee you will receive not only that update, but four more as time goes by. All the personal descriptions carry box numbers for members' protection, so that initial contacts are always in writing and via the agency.

Barbara says she doesn't insult her members by telling them how to go about writing letters, but there is a leaflet available on request. One of the pieces of advice in this leaflet is that writers should make their letters look good: *"Some things will definitely rate you as a non-starter in the relationship stakes: lined exercise or file paper; lined shorthand pad paper with perforated top edges; scraps of jotting paper; toilet paper.*"

"*You may laugh,*" says Barbara, "*but we have received letters showing all these failings.*" Greens may be sincere, but sometimes their principled neglect of appearances causes unintentional offence, as in the case of the woman who met a man whose "beard was full of egg".

However, complaints are few and far between. I spoke to Sam, 50, a careers advisor, who likes to keep his work and social life separate, and is often too busy with his own projects in the evening to go out and meet new friends. He is concerned that the traditional way of making contact, with the man approaching the woman, may sometimes offend modern women; he says it also hurts modern men to be rejected. "*With Natural Friends, at least you know the other person is interested in making contact.*" In general, he had found women with Natural Friends to be more open, and had met five female friends with whom he is still in touch. Sam admitted he was not good at following up contacts, and liked women who showed the initiative.

A couple of Natural Friends who were much quicker on the uptake are David and Siân. They met in Richmond Park one September, and were married the following May. David, 34 and divorced, joined Natural Friends when he found his Open University degree course had effectively finished off his social life. *"I wanted to meet people who like a stress-free lifestyle and the arts - those who are peaceful and not pushy,"* he says. He is a "non-fanatical green"; Siân buys recycled products and uses bottle and can banks: *"I do anything I can to help in a small way."* Their friends say they are like two peas in a pod.

PALS

This is a Welsh agency run by Barbara Elder. It offers to find partners in four types of relationship, based on the letters of its name, and described as follows: Penfriend (someone to write to or telephone), Associate (a platonic friendship), Lover (a lasting, sexual relationship) and Sweetheart (more than platonic but not too serious). As a prospective member, you choose one or two categories, but may change your mind during membership. You fill out a simple questionnaire, which gives Barbara an idea of you and the person you wish to meet, and she does the rest. She does not use a computer, nor does she invite you in for an interview, but she does encourage you to keep in touch with her by letter or phone. She usually provides between five and eight contacts over a year, but stresses that she only picks people she genuinely thinks will suit each other, so members may not be matched straight away. There is a money-back guarantee should her register not hold details of anyone compatible over the period of your membership, and the subscription is very reasonable (see page 174).

PERFECT PARTNERS

This is the largest agency based in Lancashire, and the only member of the ABIA working exclusively in the northwest. Proprietor Peter Challenor describes how he and his wife Denise came to found Perfect Partners in 1990. *"In 1989 a mutual friend of ours decided that we would make perfect partners, and so she introduced us to each other. A few months later we became engaged, and our friend asked us to return the favour and find a partner for her."* Peter and Denise were very much aware of how difficult it is to meet the right person, and the idea for their agency was born.

Within 12 months business and their reputation had grown so steadily that they were accepted into the Association of British Introduction Agencies, along with only three other agencies out of a total of 274 applicants that year. Since then they have taken over Phoenix Introductions and Top People, and started their own executive register.

Like most other agencies, they find that

men under 30 and women over 50 are more difficult to match than their other clients, and they ask patience, perseverance and understanding from anyone in those two groups wishing to join. However, no one is excluded, and once you have filled in a basic questionnaire and sent off your membership fee (see page 174), Peter and Denise invite you in for an informal meeting. All clients are interviewed personally, and clients on the executive register can request for the interview to take place in their own homes.

Peter and Denise then select a few of their clients whom they think will be compatible with you, and send you their details (photographs accompany details only if you are on the executive register). You can ring them and ask for more details, which are willingly given, except where confidentiality has been requested. Once you have decided whom you would like to meet, your details are sent to them, and they are asked to respond within 21 days. They are of course at liberty to ring the agency and request more information about you.

Once both parties are happy, Perfect Partners releases contact details, and the rest is up to you. You can ask for a list of newly registered members at intervals of not less than one month. Whether you get another shot at the members already on the books, the literature, which is sometimes absurdly pompous, doesn't make clear.

I asked Peter Challenor if he thought any of his members would like to speak to me in confidence about their experience with Perfect Partners, and he said absolutely not. He was frostily keen to impress upon me that some of the clients on their executive register are in top jobs in the public eye.

THE PICTURE DATING AGENCY

This is based in London and run by the charmingly named Mr Wright. Apart from London, it covers the southeast, the home counties and East Anglia. Most of its members are business, creative and professional people, and it is one of the few agencies with pretty equal numbers of men and women.

Jeremy Wright and his fellow director Saphel Rose, with previous careers in advertising, accountancy and public relations, have both had personal experience of dating agencies and found them to be far less considerate and caring than they claim to be. They also felt that if they had been able to see photographs of their dates beforehand, it would have saved a lot of time and disappointment meeting people to whom they were just not attracted. So they decided to start an introduction agency that used photographs and treated its clients with friendliness and respect.

The Picture Dating Agency conducts personal interviews only if you use its more expensive Gold service (see below). It uses a computer to make an initial selection of matches from a register of over 1,800 members who have filled in a fairly detailed questionnaire, then the five members of staff make a personal final selection of five people living within reasonable travelling distance of your home. You will be sent their details and photo together with names, addresses and telephone numbers, or box numbers if they have requested them. (There is no extra charge for a box number.) It is then up to you to contact those who appeal to you in writing or by phone.

Throughout the year's membership you will also be sent details of anyone who receives information about you. Although this usually adds up to quite a number of introductions, you can request extra lists of suitable members for a small fee. If you have no luck, you can change your requirements, which may have been too restrictive. If you still don't find anyone suitable, the agency will refund your subscription.

If you think you would like to join the Picture Dating Agency's Gold service, you fill in the standard questionnaire plus another sheet that gives you chance to explain more about yourself, and send these in, but with no fee at this stage. You are invited in for an interview and will be shown a file of potential partners preselected for you. If both sides are satisfied that the system will work for you, the membership fee becomes due. Your profile is forwarded to the members you have selected, and once you have both agreed to meet, you are put in touch. You can go into the office and select more people you would like to meet at any time throughout the year.

The Gold service also provides the opportunity for members to meet each other in a wine bar about once a month. Staff will perform introductions if you look lost, or leave you to find your own way if preferred. Jeremy Wright says all his members are very different, but the one thing they have in common is that they are easy-going, down-to-earth and friendly. When I asked him if he, like many agencies, had a problem finding partners for women over 40, he said no, but it did get more difficult over the age of 50. For this reason, he is prepared to offer older women who want to join a substantial discount, and he offers the same to anyone unemployed.

I was impressed with what I found out about this agency. Its Gold service is very similar to that offered by the higher-profile Drawing Down the Moon, but costs a fraction of the price.

Leo, a 41-year-old solicitor, is a member of the Gold service, and is now in the second relationship that he has begun through this agency. His first friend has also gone back on the books to find a new partner. Leo told me that he had always found it difficult to meet women in London. *"I had tried this sort of thing before: I'd put an ad in* Time Out *and had a go at Dateline, but I found both methods a bit hit-and-miss."* I asked him about Picture Dating's parties, and he said that he was amazed at how many attractive people of both sexes went to them. *"All the social events are relaxed and friendly and Jeremy Wright, who runs them, has always remembered my name right from the start."*

Stephen is also with Picture Dating. He is a photographer in a male-orientated industry and travels abroad a lot for his work, so he hardly ever gets to meet new women. He tried

Dateline, and found it "unsophisticated". *"Picture Dating is a modern, intelligent and civilized way of meeting people - it's the '80s and '90s way. No one there is short of friends or short of people to go out with, they are just looking for someone different. "* He chose Picture Dating because its questionnaire *"gives people a chance to express themselves - it's more than just ticking a box. "* He also thinks the photograph helps in narrowing down the choice: *"There's no point in pretending that looks aren't important. "*

Stephen met three women through Picture Dating before finding Kathy, with whom he is blissfully happy. They do tell their close friends how they met, but Kathy sometimes finds it embarrassing to talk about. Stephen says: *"She is very shy, a very private person, and I think it took a lot of courage for her to join an agency. "* Kathy's courage has paid off, and changed two lives for the better.

SARA EDEN INTRODUCTIONS

This is a nationwide service run from a 300-

year-old building opposite Windsor Castle in Berkshire. This expensive and upmarket bureau has won itself a reputation as the agency that caters for beautiful people.

Being beautiful and successful can be a problem, says its principal, Karen Mooney. Far from being the magnet that most people would suppose, good looks, faultless grooming and conspicuous evidence of wealth in personal taste can be daunting to the opposite sex. Beautiful people of both sexes are always expected to have partners already, and if they are discovered to be single, they are treated with suspicion, as if they must automatically have some terrible personality defect. Often, people of average looks do not take beautiful people seriously, Karen explains. Gorgeous men and women are assumed always to be on the prowl, rather than looking for commitment, and they are rarely credited with sensitivity or intelligence.

High-earning and ambitious women who are also stunningly attractive often find it triply difficult to meet men who will appreciate them as human beings. One such member of Sara Eden says: *"There's no such thing as the New Man, just a lot of old men - some of them very young - who want the same old thing ... a decoration on their arm. They don't want competition from intelligent women. Nothing has changed and the more successful a woman becomes, the harder she finds it to meet a kindred spirit."*

Sara Eden has an imaginative questionnaire and employs a team of trained consultants who conduct personal interviews with all its clients. One thing that Karen Mooney likes to find out is whether you are looking for a person who will be your own mirror imagine or your complementary opposite. She describes the ideal relationship as being like a figure of eight: *"two rounded people who come together and interlock"*.

The bureau does not take anyone who applies to join, as all new members must have something to appeal to the 1,000 already on the register. Not all the men are hunks, but smaller men tend to be big achievers, says Karen. And not all the women are top executives; many are pretty hairdressers or air hostesses.

Personal profiles, complete with photographs, are there in her office for members to leaf through: initially, and with the help of the staff who have a personal knowledge of the members from their interviews, new recruits may select from six to 15 people whom they would like to meet. Then your profile and photograph are sent to them, and if they like what they see and read, telephone numbers are disclosed and you get in touch.

Many agencies never find out how successful they are, because their clients just melt away into the sunset together without telling them, but Karen knows that she has at least a one in seven success rate, and she expects to get invited to around 40 weddings a year.

VEGETARIAN MATCHMAKERS

This is situated in the heart of alternative London - Crouch End - from where it provides a nationwide service for vegetarians, vegans and like-minded people who want to make contact for love and friendship, with either or both sexes, or to find travelling or business partners in green schemes, flatmates or alternative therapists. In addition to its main service, VMM runs weekends away, in the UK and abroad, and has a busy programme of social gatherings and occasional big parties - and not just in London.

In response to your request, VMM sends you some very positive literature about itself, including rave reviews from press and members, and a few samples of pen-portraits, to help you compile your own. Your portrait written, you specify the age group and gender you wish to meet, and for a small fee, you're in. You receive lists of VeggieMembers as requested, and your profile is circulated for as long as you like, up to one year. Your mailing is printed out especially for you, and VMM promises that it will not be a muddled, out-of-date sheaf of non-selective photocopies. The agency aims to save time, frustration and trees by getting it right with each printing. Updates are sent to you when you request them. VMM has over 500 members: some give their phone numbers and others can be contacted only via the bureau. The bureau does not charge for forwarding letters or cassettes to its members, and it never divulges their addresses.

This is an exceptionally reasonably priced, friendly and efficient service, and putting the accent on sharing a common lifestyle takes much of the stress out of finding a partner. VMM gives a feeling that the search itself will be enjoyable and that there will be all sorts of unexpectedly beneficial twists and turns on the way.

My Choice

Having completed a survey of introduction agencies, I'm bound to be asked which is the best. The answer is that no "best" can be recommended for everyone, as the choice is so wide and each prospective member should pick the agency she or he feels most comfortable with. However, my own preference would be for an agency where the highest priority is placed on personal warmth. The client is looking for happiness, and the best an agency can offer is a service that combines a realistic attitude with real warmth and understanding.

My first choice for personal service would be the Katharine Allen marriage bureau (page 58), because the principal, Mrs Halson, has genuine warmth of character, which spills over into the delightful premises in which she works. Here is a woman, I felt, who didn't wake up one morning thinking: *"What can I do to make money? I know, I'll open an introduction agency."* She is actually interested in people (which helps - not all of them are, even though they pretend to be!), and matching them up is something she finds endlessly fascinating. However, I do have a reservation: this is a marriage bureau. I think it would make it less easy for me to appreciate the partners I was matched up with if I started from the first meeting to imagine what it would be like to be married to them. I would prefer to think of any meeting as having open-ended prospects.

Katharine Allen is nationwide, but if I lived in London or the southeast, I might well choose the Picture Dating Agency (page 113). This is one of only three agencies I came across where the client goes into the office and is allowed to riffle through the books to pick potential partners - most agencies don't let you loose on the opposite sex in this way. Picture Dating also welcomes women in their forties. Its service seems to me no less comprehensive than that of the higher-profile Drawing Down the Moon, but at about a third of the price, it is certainly a better buy. And where Drawing Down the Moon is professional to its fingertips, I have to say that perversely, I find the slightly less-in-control Jeremy Wright, principal of Picture Dating, more reassuring. He is certainly well liked by his members. Whenever I have spoken to him on the phone he has seemed slightly breathless, and once admitted to being hungover from a Picture Dating party the night before, which recommended him to me as someone who throws himself into his job heart, soul and liver. At Picture Dating's parties, by the way, members do not wear name badges, as they do at social evenings thrown by Drawing Down the Moon.

If I lived in the north, I would have no hesitation in joining Friendships, run by Jennifer Stacey (page 93). This is a very reasonably priced agency with a superfluity of men, and could be an excellent choice for the single mother. I liked Jennifer's down-to-earth attitude and her sense of humour. She told me about the dating experience of a snobbish acquaintance of hers, who asked an agency to fix her up with a businessman, and got all dressed up in her finery to find her date waiting for her at the appointed spot in his own ice-cream van.

There are two nationwide listings agencies that appealed to me: Natural Friends (page 106) and Vegetarian Matchmakers (page 121). Both are among the cheapest agencies in the ABIA, and both offer an excellent, friendly and informal service. These are good agencies to join if you find the search for a partner makes you feel self-conscious and vulnerable, as the accent is on friendship based on a common interest in all things green, rather than on romance.

ENGLISH ROSE

One of the most startling stories I came across while writing this book happened through an agency called English Rose, which is in Margate (tel 0843 290735). English Rose is not a member of the ABIA - presumably because it's a transatlantic organization that doesn't seem to think much of the British male - so I haven't featured it in the main body of the chapter, but this story is worth telling.

Laura was an unwanted baby and lived in children's homes until she was eight, when she was reunited with her parents. But there was no happiness at home, and she moved into a hostel while she was in her teens. It was there that she met her Thai husband. They married when Laura was 19, and had two daughters, but parted shortly after the birth of the second. Eight years later Laura was feeling lonely for a mate, but her life as a single mother was giving her little opportunity to meet new people. Then she saw an advert for English Rose, an agency that matches British women with "all-American gentlemen". English Rose says: *"If you have ever dreamed of starting a new life in the United States with a financially secure attractive gentleman as your lifelong companion, then we could be the answer to your dream. American gentlemen have that unique combination of charm, generosity and consideration so often lacking in their British counterparts. If you like to be spoiled, pampered and treated like a lady, then you will certainly appreciate the American Male!"*

This oozing prose took Laura's fancy so much that she sold her typewriter to raise the £450 membership fee. (Men on the other side of the Atlantic have to pay more than twice that much to join. According to English Rose, they think it's worth it to secure a wife who is "demure, cultured and refined".)

Anyway, among Laura's first batch of introductions was a man called Elliot, whose surname went rather nicely with Laura's, and she plucked up the courage to phone him. Elliot had a clerical job at the Pentagon. He was shy, reserved and very polite, and had also had a history of unfulfilling relationships behind him. The warmth and friendliness in Laura's voice appealed to him enormously.

The seeds of love were sown immediately, and in very fertile ground on both sides. Letters and photographs were exchanged. The couple found that not only did they share similar experiences, but that their looks appealed: both are tall, dark and striking. In only their third phone conversation they found themselves saying they loved each other. Elliot says: *"I gave her some big explanation about how I don't often say those words and when I do, it really means something, then I said: 'I love you.' Laura was real quiet and I thought: Oh no. I really blew it this time! But then I heard her crying and she said: 'I love you too!'"*.

Both of them realized the danger of falling

in love before they'd even met: how could it possibly be true? Under the circumstances, the stress they felt before their first meeting was far worse than what precedes most blind dates. Within two months of the first phone call, Elliot was on a plane to Heathrow. He had the strain of a long-haul flight; Laura had the strain of waiting: she was at the airport three hours before his plane arrived at 6 a.m.

Elliot tried to calm himself with a drink. He felt hot and very nervous. The moments before they first saw each other must have been agonising. Laura was in a state of extreme anxiety: *"I nearly died when I saw the flight had landed and the luggage was in the hall. I was sure my legs were going to give way."* As Elliot approached the barrier, he recognized her immediately: *"She was the only person on the wrong side of the barrier and looked as though she was having a heart attack. I was really worried. She had her hands up in front of her face and she was crouching down. I thought: I'd better get there quick before she collapses."*

He put his arms around her and almost

carried her to a seat. They were both overcome, and totally oblivious of everything but each other. They sat there a long time, just gazing at each other and hugging, laughing and crying and touching each other's faces, trying to turn the fantasy into reality. It must have been an experience to break all records on the stress scale.

Christina Rhodes, who runs English Rose, was not surprised - as I must say I was - to find that Elliot and Laura remained delighted with each other for the whole of Elliot's visit. Ms Rhodes, who used to run an agency where people were matched according to their astrological signs, has about 7,000 names on her files - 3,000 British women and 4,000 American men - and says it's unusual for a week to go by without hearing of two or three weddings from matches she has made. She says: *"We're dealing with business and professional men who can afford to fly their partners out to the States if the relationship gets that far, and we make sure our ladies are well presented and able to hold an intelligent conversation.* "

That last remark would be enough to put me right off Ms Rhodes's agency, but English Rose worked for Laura and Elliot. After Elliot had returned home, they agreed that Laura would wait for her divorce to come through before she and her two daughters flew out to join him, and that they would limit their phone conversations to five minutes, and sometimes just allow the phone to ring three times, as a signal for "I love you". But they didn't stick to any of their resolutions, and some of their phone calls lasted up to six hours. The only sensible thing to do was for Laura to join Elliot as soon as possible. Within a week Laura had sold what she couldn't take with her, arranged for the rest to be shipped out, and she and her two young daughters were on the plane. In the meantime, Elliot had rented a cheaper and bigger house for them all 100 miles from his work. But the prospect of commuting such a great distance every day didn't bother him, because the rest of their lives had begun.

Chapter Five

DATING BY NUMBERS - COMPUTERS THAT PLAY CUPID

Everyone has heard of Dateline and seen pictures of Roy and Wendy, Barry and Jean, and Ian and Shereena, cuddling on a garden swing, laughing in a cornfield or gazing into each other's eyes over a glass of champagne: living proof of the Dateline slogan "You too can find love".

Dateline, the oldest established and the biggest computer dating agency, says it's for everyone: it has over 35,000 members, with 3,000 more joining each month. Ring the Dateline number (see page 174) and they'll send you an introductory pack: information, a questionnaire, and a book of true stories of Dateline romance.

What Sort Of People Join Dateline?

The typical story in the Dateline book takes you from slumping in an armchair at home with a streaming cold wondering if you have the energy to clear up the kids' toys, to sitting up in bed in a luxury hotel in Tenerife drinking champagne on ice with the man of your dreams. Dateline people, it seems from their publicity material, are romantic traditionalists. The family's approval of the new partner plays a key role, there are plenty of red roses, and in more than one story the man actually goes down on bended knee to propose.

Dateline says its members may be any age from 18 to 70 and come from all walks of life. They are farmers, engineers, salesmen, computer programmers, stockbrokers, nurses, MPs, chemists, musicians, titled people and even zoo keepers. Around 30 per cent are graduates.

How Does It Work?

First you complete the questionnaire, ticking boxes to build up a personal profile, and a profile of the person you want to meet. The first part of the questionnaire establishes basic facts such as height, build, age and educational background. The remainder deals with personality, interests and attitudes. In addition, the questionnaire for the more expensive Dateline Gold service gives members the chance to write something about themselves and attach a photograph. All information is of course confidential.

On receipt of your completed questionnaire and a cheque for a year's membership (see page 174), your details are fed into the computer. Gold customers are invited in for an interview and are allocated to a consultant: personal contact is maintained throughout the membership, which explains the higher fee.

Within days, Dateline sends you your first "matching run": a computer printout of six compatible people in the area of your choice. Names, addresses and phone numbers are supplied, but no other details. It's up to you to get in touch and find out more, though Dateline will reveal occupations if you give them a ring. Your name may also come up on other people's runs, unless you specify otherwise.

You can request an unlimited number of runs during your membership; each additional run costs £5. At the end of the year, you have the option of renewing your membership for a reduced fee. Dateline's Frances Pyne says she has high hopes of people meeting someone with whom they want to start a relationship within the first three runs. Around 1,000 people a year ask to have their names taken off the computer because they have met their match, but she believes that many more are suited and quietly go their own way.

Dateline has its own monthly publication, the only magazine aimed specifically at this market. It features around 20 pages of personal adverts - fascinating to read. Some have photographs, and there are more men than women. A copy comes free in your introductory pack from Dateline.

THE LUCK OF THE DRAW

The Dateline questionnaire was devised with the help of a number of psychologists, and has been refined over the years to produce what must be the most efficient and accurate way of matching personality types a computer can achieve.

Personally, I don't like answering questionnaires. I particularly disliked this one because ticking boxes puts people into pigeon-holes and gives no scope for individuality. I imagined that putting "no" to a whole range of social activities including parties, pubs, clubs, discos and dinner parties would mean that I got paired up with someone who said "yes" to number 163: *On the whole do you prefer an evening in watching television?* (to which I answered another gloomy "no"). And how could anyone answer this one: *"Are you (tick box) always, sometimes, or never intellectual?"*

Many of the questions held no relevance for me one way or the other, so my answers gave a miserable picture of my character (though an accurate one by the computer's standards), and I was not unduly surprised to find myself matched in my first run with a worker at the nuclear power station that I was campaigning to have shut down. I spoke to other people who had had a similar experience: verdicts on Dateline included "unsophisticated" and "a mixed bag".

The lesson to learn here is that you should only join an agency where they get the questions right *for you*, and not struggle to fit your personality to their requirements. The many people who have found happiness through Dateline will undoubtedly have felt a lot more comfortable than I did answering its questions.

My experiment with Dateline's magazine was more successful. Through it I exchanged letters with several men from very different walks of life, including a psychologist and a breeder of budgerigars, and I eventually met four of my correspondents. The first was J, who described himself as "an entrepreneur with green interests". He had sent me a selection of photographs of himself. "Me in Belize" showed a weatherbeaten figure in shorts and a shirt with buttons and flaps, hung about with cameras, and with one foot on a fallen tree trunk and one hand on his hip: very handsome. In "Relaxing in Honolulu" he was sprawling crumpled, with a tall drink, in front of palm trees; while "At a friend's wedding" had him in a white jacket with a dark carnation, dispensing champagne in a conservatory.

Unfortunately, I knew the second I saw J that I would never sip mulled wine in his inglenook, and when I asked him about his "green interests", he told me he imported artefacts made of tropical hardwood. I couldn't help wondering if he had got the wrong end of the stick.

The next one I met was a Shakespearean actor, and this was a fascinating experience, because I had never been in the company of a professional actor before. R did all the talking, which was mostly about himself, and mostly about how his talents were not sufficiently recognized, so that he always ended up with minor parts. His talents seemed considerable to me: he rolled his eyes, bared his teeth and flared his nostrils as he talked, and throwing his head back and spreading his arms, he embraced in his complaint all the other diners in the Indian restaurant where we sat. His work made it difficult for him to have any kind of social life, but I think what he was really looking for was not a partner, but an audience.

The third man I met was a shepherd, an extremely nice man, tall, gentle and diffident, with a shy sense of humour. I liked him very much, but we had little common ground for conversation. I am interested in sheep, and we talked about them at length, but finally there was no more to ask. While I told him a little about myself, he gazed at me with a bemused unreal look in his eye, as if I was speaking in an exotic tongue. We parted with friendly wishes on both sides, and on mine, the conviction that he would make someone a very good husband.

Finally, I met a graphic designer. L was also a marathon runner, he had previously been married to a German, and he enjoyed looking at paintings. I liked his photograph. We corresponded some more, and had promising conversations on the phone. When we met, I did not recognize him from his photograph, which turned out to be several years old. (Always send a recent photograph to avoid seeing someone's face fall.) My overwhelming impression was one of being engulfed in aftershave. Expecting an artistic athlete, I found instead a natty dresser no longer slim with a precision haircut and wearing jewellery. Goodness knows what he thought of me, but the lack of chemistry, after high expectations, hung heavily in the air.

Disappointment was short-lived, however. And though I did not see any of my Dateline men more than once, I was glad of the experience of meeting them. I found the whole business very absorbing, and I learned a lot about my own perceptions and misconceptions.

Meeting new members of the opposite sex in this way, for a drink that can lead without pressure to a meal, makes a refreshing change, and if you feel your life could be more eventful, it certainly adds novelty and spice. How else could I possibly - within the course of one week - have found myself visiting an otter sanctuary with a shepherd and eating curry with Banquo's ghost?

Date-Link is Scotland's own answer to Dateline, with a head office in Helensburgh and subsidiary offices in Edinburgh and Glasgow. As with Dateline, there is a form to fill in with boxes to tick, and a map overlaid with a grid - this time covering all of Scotland and its islands - on which you mark out the square or rectangle within which you would be prepared to travel to meet people.

ANOTHER EXPERIENCE

One Dateline member I talked to was Lara. Lara is a solicitor in her fifties; she is funny and lively, and most of her friends are younger. She met six men through the Dateline computer, all of whom were retired, and a little ponderous. These elderly seeming men were looklng for someone to replace the traditional stay-at-home wives who had divorced them: a prospect that made Lara recoil. She felt that the computer was selecting her matches primarily on age, and not taking into account the fact that she was by nature youthful and outgoing. For Lara, Dateline was a depressing experience: she was sure there were lively men in their late forties or fifties who would want to meet her, but the computer was ccrtainly not putting them in touch.

Chapter Six

WISH YOU WERE HERE -
SINGLES HOLIDAYS

There are many people, and I count myself among them, who actively enjoy living alone, but it seems that very few of us like to go on holiday by ourselves. Holidays are for sharing.

The English Tourist Board says that 84 per cent of single people holidaying in the UK do it with friends or relatives. Of that number, there must be many who would also like holidays - at home and abroad - to be for making new friendships, but have shirked away from the idea of a singles holiday in the belief that it would turn out to be either a lager-soaked orgy or a group of depressingly untalented people taking instruction in watercolour.

Fifteen years ago, when to go on a singles holiday felt like admitting you were desperate,

I was impressed when the very shy woman I worked for steeled herself to try one. She arrived back in the office after only a few days, explaining that she'd had more of a singles holiday than she'd bargained for, because the sun-drenched villa she was to have shared with fifteen other people had been empty - except for herself.

Things have improved. Today the range of holidays aimed specifically to appeal to the single traveller (a group that represents 22 per cent of the holiday market) has never been greater. There is plenty to inspire: a gourmet weekend - a gorilla safari - a cycle tour in China - a walk through North Borneo. All you have to do is choose (which may prove difficult enough), then look forward to enjoying the experience, with the added bonus of sharing it with like-minded people in a similar situation to yourself.

There is no doubt that friendships do blossom in the holiday atmosphere. M, a singer in her mid-thirties, told me that she now lives with a man she met on a cycling holiday in New

England. When the holiday ended, she thought they would probably not see one another again, because they lived at opposite ends of England. But they found they could not bear to be apart, and within three weeks, he had moved in with her. Two years on, they are still cycling.

Specialists In The Singles Market

SOLO'S HOLIDAYS (081 202 0855) measure their success by their sociability. The organizers try to get a good mix, and there are two age groups: 30+ (for women up to 49 and men up to 54) and 50+. The company offers a very comprehensive range of tours and weekend breaks, in this country and all over the world. Bon viveurs can join an Elizabethan banquet at Hatfield House, or spend Christmas and New Year in traditional style in Edinburgh or Brighton; for the energetic, there are weekends rambling and playing tennis, squash and badminton. Short-haul holidays take you skiing in Switzerland, golfing in Spain, or learning to dive in the Red Sea. Long-haul tours include China (the Great Wall), South America (the Rio carnival), the Seychelles (wildlife) and Africa (on safari).

Solo's books single rooms to avoid the single room supplement. It says its typical first-time holidaymaker is "apprehensive", even "petrified". Some weekenders almost leave before the welcome cocktail party, thinking they must be "mad" to have come. Only hours later they are saying: "This is marvellous - why did I wait so long?" and: "Can't wait to book up again." Try a weekend first to see if they get it right for you. Solo's advertises in Dateline's magazine, as does LONGSTAFF LEISURE HOLIDAYS (0756 760246), run by Sylvia Longstaff at Hartrigg, a Victorian country house in the Yorkshire Dales. Sylvia says her house party holidays always end in tears, because no one wants to go home. She offers every country comfort from tea in bed and home-cooked food to long walks, sightseeing (York and the Brontës' home at Haworth), barbecues and a folk night. Optional extras include pony trekking and abseiling. Rooms are shared: Sylvia says no one would come down to dinner on the first night if they weren't, and it's good for breaking the ice. Making friends is what these weekends and short breaks are all about, and many of the guests have become regulars. There are often more women than men, but Longstaff Leisure has launched 32 marriages since it started up in 1983, and Sylvia's own partner was one of her first guests. Included in the introductory material is a list of names and phone numbers of people who have spent a holiday at Hartrigg and would be pleased to talk to apprehensive potential guests.

SMALL WORLD (0293 599966), part of the Sovereign group, takes the house-party idea abroad. Its locations are Portugal, France, Italy, Greece and Turkey, and you can join a party of up to 25 in a villa or cruise on a caïque: a traditional wooden sailing boat with a motor and cabins for up to 18. Accommodation is shared, unless you wish to pay extra. Guests are usually in their thirties and forties, and there tend to be more women than men. Each group is looked after by a host and/or hostess, who provide a substantial continental breakfast with cheese, fruit and yoghurt, and one three-course meal a day with unlimited wine. The villas sometimes have a tennis court and usually a swimming pool, and no one will mind if you lounge by it all day and do nothing, though there are sights to explore and windsurfing and diving on offer. There is a relaxed atmosphere and the holidaymakers usually make their own plans, though your host will organize an outing if you wish.

THE IMAGINATIVE TRAVELLER (071 792 8494) is a company that specializes in taking groups of 10-25 people to the Middle East (Egypt, Israel, Jordan and Turkey) and India and Nepal. The idea is to allow the single traveller to enjoy an adventurous and companionable holiday without all the frustrations and difficulties that travelling alone or with a friend in these countries might normally bring. Accommodation may be anything from a maharajah's palace to a budget hotel (chosen for economy, cleanliness and character) or a tent (all equipment provided).

Itineraries are packed and varied and offer many excursions off the beaten track, taking in thermal springs, elephants, camels, traditional sailing boats, diving in the Red Sea, cycling and a jeep safari to see lions and flamingos. However, the company is flexible, and invites you to invent your own holiday: it can organize flights, accommodation, meals and even an escort. The Imaginative Traveller holds regular film nights at its Chiswick office: informal evenings at which anyone interested can find out more about the holidays and meet prospective fellow-travellers.

EXODUS (081 673 0779) is a company that specializes in adventure holidays on foot or overland in expedition trucks. Most of their treks are in the world's high mountain areas (as far afield as the Himalayas, China, former Soviet Union and South America), well away from civilization and tourist facilities, and guarantee healthy exercise and magnificent scenery. The treks are graded from easy to very tough, and tour leaders take care of groups of up to 15 people, who may be any age from 17 to 70. On most treks, Exodus looks after porterage, making and breaking camp, and all the camp chores and cooking, though on some of its European tours, walkers are expected to pitch in to some extent.

Its overland tours go all over the world, including to Africa, Asia, Latin America, China and Alaska. Total comfort is not guaranteed on all tours, but the ruggedness is part of the attraction. Some expeditions, such as the 23-week African Discoverer, promise desert heat, muddy and near-impassable trails, tropical rainstorms and hard ground to sleep on, as well as extraordinary scenery from mountains to rainforests, and the greatest concentration of wildlife in the world. There are less demanding and shorter adventures, but on the whole, the Exodus holiday is not for the couch potato.

NOT EXCLUSIVELY SINGLES, BUT SINGLES WELCOME AND OFTEN IN ABUNDANCE

EXPLORE (0252 319 448) takes groups of around 18 people, most of whom are between 25 and 55, and about half of whom are single travellers, on unusual tours to an impressive range of countries. It visits places tourists would not normally penetrate, such as remote Berber villages in the Atlas Mountains, where travellers stay in the homes of local people. Explore aims to leave the planet as it found it, and donates a percentage of its profit to the World Wildlife Fund for Nature. It divides its adventures into eight categories.

"Cultural adventures" focus on local crafts, ethnic peoples and classic sites. The "wildlife and natural history" section offers safaris and bushwalking. Those going on "ethnic encounters" to meet the Tuaregs, the Maya or the Pygmies, are told that the aim of their visit is to help spread tolerance and understanding between peoples and races, with the minimum of cultural and environmental disturbance. "Easy to moderate hiking" offers the opportunity to walk from village to village through open countryside, while your luggage is transported to your next resting place, while "major treks" tackle higher altitudes for strong mountain walkers. "Wilderness experience" visits deserts and rainforests, "sail and seatreks" use native craft to explore rivers and archipelagos, and "raft and river journeys" take place anywhere from the Dordogne to the Amazon.

Explore runs slide shows around the country so people can find out more about small group adventure travel and discover who their travelling companions are likely to be. Staff say that over 60 per cent of bookings come from people who have already been on an Explore holiday, or who have been personally recommended.

CONTIKI (081 290 6777) is a company that caters for 18-35-year-olds. Around half of its clients are travelling solo, and are encouraged to agree to room-sharing with one or two others (reductions for triple sharing). The Contiki brochure invites "pleasure-seekers for non-stop, get-up-and-go, dream-filled touring" to many destinations worldwide. The accent is on activity, and the Contiki holidaymaker is likely to be constantly on the move, on whistle-stop tours of his or her chosen country. For example, one American tour takes in San Francisco, Yosemite, Las Vegas, Grand Canyon, Phoenix, Tijuana, San Diego and Los Angeles, all in 10 days. No stone is left unturned: an aquatic show with killer whales, a barbecue on the beach, a desert drive, Montezuma's castle, a helicopter in the Grand Canyon (optional extra), casinos, pine chalets, jet- and water skiing are all on offer as well as nightlife enough to satisfy the most committed raver.

TWENTYS (061 237 3333) promises pure unadulterated fun to the right people: "no muppets, no screaming sprogs and no dreary souls". This is the company for "people like yourself who want to leave Snoresville behind for sun, fun, thrills and some of the most happenin' nightlife on the planet". Of course you have to be under 30 to appreciate "the most kickin' wicked two weeks of the year in the hottest spots of Europe", but if you want "a crazy lifestyle" and "one helluva hardcore holiday" in a place that's "fit to bust with bars", then Twentys is your company. Everything is done to attract the single traveller, and there are discounts for parties of three friends willing to share a room and other holidays with "zero supplements on single rooms", or where one in eight or one in ten goes free. Holidays are definitely hedonistic, with swimming pools to lounge by the morning after the night before, and special events like a banquet where you "eat and drink medieval-style to the sound of the Four Tops", but there are jet-skis etc. for those who want to do more than party away the "stonkingly awesome nightlife".

ALTERNATIVE HOLIDAYS

EARTHWATCH (0865 311 600) offers unique working holidays for those whose interest is the environment. Its adverts say tourists need not apply: it promises adventure, friendship, challenge and growth, and "a feeling of personal fulfilment that you may remember for the rest of your life".

Earthwatch is a charitable organization that works rather like Voluntary Service Overseas. It supports research and projects all over the world and recruits "volunteers", who pay to join them for upwards of a fortnight. You could find yourself tracking whales in the Canary Islands or helping to rehabilitate orphaned orang-utans in the rainforest. Other projects cater for interests in botany, anthropology or archaeology. During their stay in their chosen country, volunteers live in informal lodges and camps and eat local food prepared by local cooks. Earthwatch has members from all over the world, of all ages, and from all walks of life, and if you share their common concern for the planet, this could be the holiday for you.

WORKING WEEKENDS ON ORGANIC FARMS (WWOOF, 0273 476286) is a non-profit-making organization that provides voluntary workers with first-hand experience in any aspect of organic farming and gardening, from bee keeping, through hedge laying, to peat cutting, seaweed spraying and rearing kids and ducklings. For a small fee, you can join WWOOF, and you will be sent a bi-monthly newsletter that lists places needing help on particular weekends, as well as job opportunities in the organic movement. You pay your own travel costs and take a sleeping bag, but full board and lodging is provided in the farmhouse or outbuildings in exchange for two eight-hour days' work. Vegetarians are welcome. Ask how many other volunteers you are likely to meet on the weekend of your choice: it could be up to 15.

Working Holidays is published with a yearly update by the Central Bureau for Educational Visits and Exchanges (071 486 5101). This comprehensive, highly readable and very well produced paperback guide is also available from bookshops and gives details of short- and longer-term job opportunities in many countries throughout the world and in many areas: vegetable harvesting, yacht crewing, heritage restoration, summer camp counselling, waterfront instructors, ecology project work, community work, catering, farmwork, and couriers, to name but a few.

Other guides to voluntary work are *Volunteer Work* by Hilary Sewell (same publisher as above), and *The International Directory of Voluntary Work*, published by Vacation Work.

Cultural Holidays

ARCHITECTURAL TOURS (081 341 1371) arranges study visits all over the world for people interested in 20th-century architecture. Many of its participants are working architects. Architectural Tours also has a UK programme of lectures and exhibitions and organizes visits to houses designed and lived in by architects, which it says are extremely popular.

MARTIN RANDALL TRAVEL (081 994 6477) organizes tours to cultural centres in Europe and beyond to the Near East that take in art, architecture, archaeology and music. The tours are meticulously planned and led by a highly qualified lecturer chosen for scholarship, communicative skills and companionability. A substantial proportion of Martin Randall's clients are single, many in their fifties. Roomshare is recommended, though single rooms are available with a supplementary charge. Groups are kept small, usually under 22. Travel and accommodation are comfortable, with hotels usually 3- or 4-star, sometimes 5-star. Travellers are provided with a list of recommended reading when booking, and also with historical notes. With Martin Randall you can spend Christmas in Vienna, or Prague, or in the Sahara, and New Year in Umbria. Summer tours include Monet and the Landscapes of Impressionism, Art and Medicine in Bologna and Padua, and Art and Wine in Burgundy.

With PROSPECT MUSIC AND ART TOURS (081 995 2151) you can choose from a fascinating range of tours that includes Art in the South of France, Writers' Paris, and Turkish Carpets. On this last tour, the group visits the outstanding collection of Seljuk and early Ottoman rugs in Istanbul, before travelling into the rug-making regions in the west of Turkey to see dyeing, weaving and even a silk cocoon market, in the company of a lecturer-guide who has studied Turkish and

Persian and worked as a carpet restorer. What could be more fascinating? Prospect also offers an attractive programme of music and opera at various centres including Vienna, New York, Milan and Munich. The majority of Prospect's clients are single, there are more women than men, and the average age is around 50, but Prospect is keen to attract younger clients of both sexes.

ACE STUDY TOURS (0223 835 055) is run by the Association for Cultural Exchange, which cooperates with universities and adult education organizations in the UK and abroad. The brochure offers a very wide selection of tours, covering art and architectural history, archaeology, geology, music, theatre, ecology and wildlife. Tours aim to combine three elements: the study of interesting subjects, pleasant venues, and stimulating leaders. ACE donates about £20,000 a year to educational projects, such as literacy in South India, nature conservation programmes, and a study on the impact of tourism in Nepal.

ACE tours include Wild Flowers of High Aragon; Italian Lakes, Villas and Gardens; Prague Music Festival; The Mayas in Guatemala; Scottish Castles and Palaces; and Ancient Lycia. About one-quarter of ACE travellers are single, and there is a single room supplement. The brochure points out that many single rooms tend to be inferior to double rooms, and the supplement pays for privacy rather than comfort. Most single travellers are women, and the age range tends to be fifties.

CYCLING

BIKE EVENTS and BIKE TOURS (0225 480130 or 310859) are sister companies that offer cyclists a whole range of opportunities from one-day events (such as the London to Brighton bike ride), to touring holidays in the UK or in countries as far flung as China, Hungary, Kenya and America. The tours are promised to be a marvellous blend of sightseeing, exploration, peace, relaxation, fun and socializing. Daily mileages are well within most people's abilities and the routes are carefully researched to take you and your bike in an unhurried way through the quietest, most beautiful parts of your chosen country.

The exercise guarantees enjoyment of the local cuisine. Vegetarians are catered for, and UK Bicycle Beanos, one of their categories of holidays, offer exclusively vegetarian and vegan food. The holidays are hotel or camping based, and can be as quiet or as sociable as you like. You can set off each day in your own time, and cycle with a group, or alone if you choose. Camping gear and luggage is carried by the support vehicle and a nurse and a mechanic are on hand if needed. Bike hire is an option on most trips: the state of your bike is considered by the organizers to be more important than your level of fitness, though some tours - for example, through the Pyrenees - do require more than average stamina.

SAILING AND SKIING

Skiing holidays have always been popular with single people and groups of friends, as the activity on the slopes breaks the ice and the après-ski melts it in the convivial atmosphere of a hotel bar or a chalet. Many different companies offer such holidays (look in the back pages of the Sunday papers), one being OVER THE HILL (0371 856602), which goes to three resorts in France and caters for all levels of skier. Most of its clients are between the ages of 35 and 65. They aim to avoid travelling in school holidays and at weekends and have negotiated special weeks with reduced or no singles supplement. Parties are divided into small groups of the same standard, and special help is given to beginners. The organizers promise a happy and relaxed atmosphere, and a particular welcome to single travellers.

SUNSAIL (0705 210 345) has over 30 years' experience organizing sailing holidays. It operates in the Solent, with a sailing school at Emsworth near Portsmouth; in the Mediterranean; and further afield in the Caribbean and off the coast of Thailand. For singles, Sunsail recommends its Stowaway holidays, where it puts singles and couples together on skippered yachts of over 36' in size, and on its flotilla fleets. The flotillas consist of around 12 yachts, each sailed by clients, with staff to help if necessary on a lead boat, and they cruise a route of between 100 and 200 miles over 14 days.

There is no regimentation, and the chance of plenty of independent sailing to explore the myriad bays and anchorages along the route. An average day's sailing might be two to five hours, and the rest of the time could be spent swimming, sunbathing, shopping or sitting over long leisurely meals in tavernas.

With the four-strong crews of 12 boats getting together for optional social events, such as punch parties, barbecues and impromptu group dinners, there is ample opportunity to meet new friends; Sunsail puts it like this: *"Clients often become firm friends and sail together for many years afterwards."* The bigger cruising yachts, equipped with iced drinks and stereo sound, as well as snorkels, flippers etc, take a crew of six plus the skipper. No sailing experience is required for skippered yachts. On the flotillas, Sunsail aims to put at least one experienced sailor in each boat. Special dates are reserved for singles with a sprinkling of couples to make a good mix, but singles are welcome at any time of year. Sunsail also holds UK-based events at which prospective sailors can meet each other and choose their crewmates themselves.

MARK WARNER (071 938 1581) specializes in both surf and snow. In the high season this is a family-based company, but the focus shifts to singles and couples when the school holidays are over. The emphasis is on sport and après-sport socializing, which may include a game of blind date, so perhaps a Mark Warner holiday is not for the reticent. There are generally more single women than men, especially in the late 20s and early 30s age group. Summer accommodation is in beach clubs, and in winter the choice is between a chalet or a larger "clubhotel" that caters for between 50 and 100 guests paying full board.

WALKING

RAMBLERS' HOLIDAYS (0707 320 226) have been going now for 47 years and are so popular that the organization estimates that there must be over 1,000 people who have completed at least 50 tours. The tours are graded from tough to easy, but the main aim of all of them is to cater for people who like an active holiday. Ramblers go all over the world, to Turkey, Austria, Italy, Nepal, Greece, Borneo, and even along the Great Wall of China. For those who don't like the idea of lugging their belongings about on their backs, there are continuous walks, in which the ramblers proceed on foot to their next hotel while their baggage is transported ahead. Ramblers have also recently introduced a French holiday that combines walking with cooking lessons. Every holiday has a leader, though unless you are following a fixed itinerary and moving from place to place, there is no obligation to join the leader's party. There are usually between 12 and 24 people in a group, and shared interests and the exertion of walking mean that friendly informality is quickly achieved, bypassing the necessity for social chit-chat.

WORLDSAWAY (0373 858956) is another company that offers adventure to people keen on using their leg power. Its walking holidays and mountain treks are designed to appeal to walkers of all abilities who want to explore the magnificent scenery of the Himalayas, Morocco, Turkey, Iceland, Greenland, South America or East Africa. You do not have to be an athlete or a mountaineer to enjoy yourself, though some of the more rugged high altitude treks do require full fitness and previous experience. There are rest days for acclimatization where necessary, and for relaxation and exploration.

Trips are scheduled to take advantage of clear weather, spring and summer flowers, bird and animal migrations and religious festivals. Accommodation is in hotels (single supplements are avoided where possible) and in tents; all luggage is transported for you by porters, yaks or ponies, so all you need to carry is perhaps a sweater, your camera and a bottle of water. Trcks are led by an experienced tour leader, though walkers move at their own pace. There are usually from 10 to 15 walkers in each group. There is no age limit - Worldsaway's oldest client was a 76-year-old who went on a 15-day trek in Langtang searching for rare rhododendrons - though most walkers are aged between 20 and 55.

Single-Parent Family Holidays

Quite a number of organizations arrange holidays for one-parent families. The advantages of such a scheme are that your children get to play with other children, activities and babysitting are often laid on, and of course you get to meet other adults in a similar situation to yourself.

S.P.L.A.S.H. (Single Parent Links and Special Holidays, 0752 674067) is a member of ABTA and also a charity. It organizes holidays mainly in holiday camps in Britain and abroad, including at Eurodisney in France and at Legoland in Denmark. A savings scheme is available for parents who cannot meet the full cost of the holiday at once, and some children may be eligible to holiday free.

GINGERBREAD (071 240 0953), the organization for single-parent families, arranges two holidays each year, during May and October, with special reductions for children.

H.E.L.P. (Holiday Endeavour for Lone Parents, 0302 725315) is a charity run by single parents that provides low cost self-catering holidays in caravans and chalets during May and September at four sites in the UK. Every year the organization aims to subsidize holidays for 25 families.

H.O.P. (Holidays for One-Parent Families, 061 370 0337) is a charity that arranges holidays, day trips and outings at discount prices. It operates a savings scheme to help spread the cost of holidays and a national befriending service that puts families in touch so that they can arrange holidays together, so reducing the cost.

HOLIDAY CARE SERVICE (0293 774 535) is a charity that provides free information and advice about holiday opportunities in the UK and abroad, not just for single parents, but also the elderly, the disabled and their carers, and those under severe financial pressures.

SINGLE TRAVELLERS PAIR UP

TRAVEL COMPANIONS (081 202 8478)

was set up by Vera Coppard and Lisa Harrison to cater for people over 30 who love to travel but hate to do it alone. In return for their membership fee, single travellers are put on a register that details their age, interests and preferred destinations, and then they are matched by Vera and Lisa with up to three prospective companions. Vera stresses that this is not a dating agency. Most of the people on the register are women, and many prefer to travel with companions of the same sex. She and Lisa make sure that non-smokers don't travel with smokers, and that people who prefer browsing in shops don't get lumbered with people who prefer browsing in art galleries, and vice versa. They have been responsible for many successful travelling partnerships, some wanting exotic independent travel, others preferring package tours, or simply weekends away to indulge their special interests.

THE ODYSSEY TRAVEL CLUB (0223 861 079) was set up in 1987, originally to find travelling partners for serious globetrotters whose friends were unavailable to go along through lack of time, money or inclination. However, the club soon found that in a world dominated by couples and families, there was little choice for the single holidaymaker who did not want to go it alone, but was too old for Club 18-30 and too young for Saga. If you are tired of paying single supplements for poky rooms, dining alone and worrying about the safety angle, Odyssey believes it has the answer. For a membership fee half that of Travelling Companions' (above), it will give you unlimited introductions to prospective travelling partners – a list of potentially suitable people arrives by return of post after completing the questionnaire. It will also send you a twice-yearly newsletter with special travel offers and hints from fellow economy-minded travellers, give discounted travel insurance and offers of weekend breaks, chalet parties etc. In addition Odyssey runs an advice line, on which members can contact people who have recently returned from the country they wish to visit, to ask about visas, climate, employment prospects etc.

ADDRESSES AND PRICES

Association of British Introduction Agencies
(ABIA),
25 Abingdon Road, London W8 6AH.
Telephone contact: Frances Pyne at Dateline.

Anglia Friendship Bureau,
Leggetts Wood, Ellough Road, Beccles,
Suffolk NR34 7AD.
Tel: 0502 715374.
Basic fee: £65.

Asian Marriage and Friendship Bureau
International,
107 Loughborough Road, Leicester LE4 5LN.
Tel: 0533 610266.
Fees: from £95 all the way up to indefinite
membership at £800.

Connections,
First Floor, 12 Market Street,
Loughborough LE11 0AA.
Tel: 0509 215031.
Fee: £140.

Country Partners,
Dingle House, Yarsop, Yazor, Herefordshire.
Tel: 0981 22437.
Fees: £190 or £220.

Dateline International,
23 Abingdon Road, London W8 6AL.
Tel: 071 938 1011.
Basic fee: £115.
Gold service: £450.
Dateline Magazine: £2 monthly from newsagents or direct.

Date-Link,
2 Marmion Avenue, Helensburgh G84 7JL.
Tel: 0436 74455.
Fee: £85.

Disdate,
76 Springfield Drive, Bromham,
Bedford MK43 8NT.
Fee: £25.

Drawing Down the Moon,
7-11 Kensington High Street,
London W8 5NP.
Tel: 071 937 8880/938 2151.
Fee: £550.

Farmers and Country Bureau,
Mere Farm, Middleton by Youlgreave,
Bakewell, Derbyshire DE4 1LX.
Tel: 0629 636281.
Fees: registration, £35.25; introductions,
£82.25; optional interview, £35.

The Friendship Bureau,
9 Wembury Road, Plymouth,
Devon PL8 8HQ.
Tel: 0752 408009.
Fees: from £38 to £75.

Friendships,
Amitie, Darrington, Pontefract WF8 3AY.
Tel: 0977 709174.
Fees: £22 for three months, £32 for six months.

Handidate Friendship Agency,
The Wellington Centre, 52 Chevallier Street,
Ipswich, Suffolk IP1 2PB.
Tel: 0473 226950.
Fee: £40.

Hand in Hand,
185 Luton Road, Dunstable,
Bedfordshire LU5 4LP.
Tel: 0582 662658.
Fees: range from £39 to £239.

Hedi Fisher Introductions,
45-46 Chalk Farm Road,
London NW1 8AJ.
Tel: 071 267 6066/485 2916.
Fees: £200, plus £250 on marriage.

Holiday Care Service,
2 Old Bank Chambers, Station Road,
Horley, Surrey RH6 9HW.
Tel: 0293 774535.

Janus Introduction Bureau,
5 Holly Grove, Tabley, Knutsford,
Cheshire WA16 OHR.
Tel: 0565 652516.
Fees range from £70 to £130.

Katharine Allen Marriage Bureau,
18 Thayer Street,
London WlM SLD.
Tel: 071 935 3115.
Fees: £400, plus £500 on marriage.

Kent Introduction Service,
83 Welland Road, Tonbridge,
Kent TN10 3TA.
Tel: 0732 770875.
Fees: £35 or £75.

Miniprints: Profile Prints,
Courtwood Film Service Ltd,
PO Box 10, Penzance,
Cornwall TR18 2BR.

Natural Friends,
15 Benyon Gardens, Culford,
Bury St Edmunds, Suffolk IP28 6EA.
Tel: 0284 728315.
Fees: £32 or £44.

PALS,
Bryn Llwyn, Babell, Holywell,
Clywd CH8 8PP.
Tel: 0352 720808.
Fees: £40 or £60.

Perfect Partners,
St Martin's Lodge,
257 Black Bull Lane, Fulwood,
Preston PR2 4YD.
Tel: 0772 718991.
Fees from £85 to £250.

The Picture Dating Agency,
29 Villiers Street, London, WC2N 6ND.
Tel: 071 839 8884/297 1424.
Fees: standard £55, Gold £120.

Sara Eden Introductions,
Eden House, 38 Thames Street,
Windsor, Berkshire SL4 1PR.
Tel: 0753 830350.
Fees: £450 or £550.

Suman Marriage Bureau,
83 South Road, Southall, Middlesex UB1 1SQ.
Tel: 081 574 4867/571 5145 (day),
081 579 2732 (weekday evenings).
Fees: £150 or £352.50;
£150 payable on marriage.

Vegetarian Matchmakers,
Century House, Nelson Road,
London N8 9RT.
Tel: 081 348 5229 (24 hours), or
Manchester (061) 973 7500 (office hours only).
Fee: £68.